You got that P.h.D.?

The Power To Scale Your Business By Focusing On The
Inputs Needed To Get The Outputs You Desire

Bobby Marhamat

ISBN: 978-0-359-23262-8

DEDICATION

This book is dedicated to all of the passionate, driven hustlers that I have met over the years. By continually learning, we can all live a better life!

CONTENTS

Introduction

Passion, Hustle, Drive (P.h.D.). Yes, for those that know me, I mention those characteristics frequently. If you want to achieve extreme success, you can't operate like everyone else. You need to operate with the P.h.D. in mind in your hiring, in how you structure your company, and in figuring out when it's time to let someone move on.

If there is one thing to remember from this book – it should be that happy employees become your most important brand ambassadors and result in bigger profits for your business. The more invested and enthusiastic people are about their work, the more passionate they are about what they are doing, the more extreme success your organization will have as a whole.

Investing in your people doesn't create a "cost" – it ensures that you:

❖ Differentiate by having a strong culture and a crew of promoters for your business.

❖ Create a competitive advantage in the marketplace.

❖ Improves and adds value to your employees, who put it right back in to the company.

❖ ...and a lot more!

I wrote this book to help all of the struggling entrepreneurs out there, the ones who've started a business and have had some success but are wondering what to do next. *How do I scale this? How can I get better? How do I build a winning culture?*

I can't lie – scaling a business is *very* hard, harder than even starting a business. Many executive leaders get it wrong by focusing on the wrong things, only to discover too late their mistakes. Of course, mistakes can help speed up the learning process, but if you experience too many of them without getting much back in return, you might find yourself in the corner.

I want to help point you in the right direction before you find yourself in that corner, fighting for the survival of the company or in a virtual tug-of-war with the investors, who are about to step in and pull the plug.

The What?

As I mentioned earlier, you've likely experienced some success with your company by capturing the interest of customers or investors (or hopefully - both!). But now you're wondering how to solidify the gains you've made and generate more revenue exponentially without incurring equally exponential costs and expenses.

The aim of this book is to remove luck and chance from your business and help you scale it quickly – but also correctly. In this book, I cover the areas that I believe are the keys to success in scaling a company.

Notice that I wrote "keys" instead of "key." There's an emphasis on the plural because I'm covering multiple areas that will form the "core" or "foundation" of your company as it scales.

Although this might sound overwhelming, you won't be doing it on your own. A portion of this book focuses on how to hire and keep employees who will be integral to the company's success... people with passion, hustle, and drive – the P.h.D.'s of employees. So, even though there's a lot of material in this book (but not a lot of fluff), once you have a strong team of employees, you'll have more hands (and brains) to help your company scale.

As you might guess, what I've written focuses almost exclusively on the internal workings of your business. Depending on your background and experience, you may already have several of these areas well under control. That's great if that's the case, though I still suggest you dip into the relevant sections to see what new bits of information you might pick up.

Why Passion-Hustle-Drive (P.h.D.)?

Here and later in this book, I want to emphasize the importance of only hiring people who demonstrate *passion*, *hustle*, and *drive*. Just so we're on the same page, here's my brief definition of each of those traits:

❖ *Passion*—An enthusiastic interest or love you have for something, which can be specific (a passion for graphic design) or general (a passion for learning).

❖ *Hustle*—Denotes urgency and the ability to not only work hard but work smart.

❖ *Drive*—The energy or ability to keep going through obstacles or failures.

By hiring only people who have P.h.D., you're setting up the right environment for a beneficial symbiosis between the workplace culture and P.h.D. employees. These employees support a positive workplace culture, which in turn feeds its energy and motivation back into the P.h.D. employees who are living it.

With such a team of highly motivated employees, there's virtually nothing you can't accomplish… though it does help to have some direction before you scale your company. That's what the rest of this book is for, so keep reading. Just remember to start every day with passion, hustle, and drive, and let that be a part of everything you do.

Why I Wrote This Book

Some fantastic experiences in my 20+ year career have led me to write this book. I have spent that time learning from some of the best minds in business and transferring that knowledge to the many people and teams that I have led. I have been fortunate to work with smart, hungry, and growth-minded individuals at every step of my career.

I recently spent the best four years of my life at Revel Systems with some of the finest people I have ever met in my life. These were *passionate*, *driven* individuals that loved what they did – and we all *hustled* to make Revel Systems the most innovative, revenue-producing product for our great customers. At Revel Systems, the people I worked with helped me realize what I mentioned earlier – it's the people with P.h.D. who drive a company's success.

After leaving Revel, I consulted for a number of companies, where I witnessed the same mistakes being made by leaders trying to scale their businesses. Through these companies, I learned to recognize what the "best" looks like. I realized that I could help other entrepreneurs with great companies scale their businesses… fast, but the right way.

I look forward to helping others create the best conditions that enable them and their employees to do their best work.

P.S. To my forever Revel family – I am humbled to have spent the time with you that I did. Continue to do your best work and live your best life.

About My Background and Experience

Some of the companies I've worked for have been big names in their industry, and some have been relatively unknown. …there probably isn't any part of a growing company that I haven't had my hands in at one time or the other.

One thing that all of my previous companies have in common is that they're involved in technology in some way, that being the topic that interests me most. I suppose technology has always captured my interest because of its changeability and potential for fast growth.

If your company doesn't happen to be in the realm of technology, don't worry! The majority of the chapters are still relevant. Chapters 10 and 11, which are about economics of a sale and revenue operations, are strongly relevant to SaaS companies. I'd still encourage you to read them, though, as you might pick up something that can be applied to your business.

High-Level Summary of Chapters

I've arranged together the chapters that are related to each other and organized them into more easily digestible "chunks." That way, depending on where you think you need the most guidance, you can just dip into that section.

As I mentioned earlier, it's great if you feel like you have certain areas of your company well under control, though I recommend at least skimming those chapters to see what new information you can pick up.

Section	Chapters
Part 1 *Readiness*	Introduction Chapter 1—Is It Time to Scale?
Part 2 *Culture*	Chapter 2—It's All About the Story! Chapter 3—Build Your Brand Chapter 4—Establish Your Core Values Chapter 5—Become Culturally Aware
Part 3 *Employees*	Chapter 6—Only Hire P.h.D.'s Chapter 7—Invest in Your People Chapter 8—Set Expectations with Performance Management
Part 4 *Sales*	Chapter 9—Build a Winning Sales Team Chapter 10—The Economics of a Sale – Get It Right! Chapter 11—Unite Your Sales Force Through Revenue Operations
Part 5 *Strategy & Adaptability*	Chapter 12—The Plans (Strategic & Operational) Chapter 13—Stay Fresh and Be Adaptable

Chapter 14 is the last chapter, and it's not assigned to any section of the book. In there, I've pulled everything together into a final message and summarized each of the chapters.

Here's what you can expect from each of the main sections of the book:

Part 1—Determine Your Readiness

To prepare for what's ahead, you need to first see where you're at. Ask yourself four key questions to decide if you're ready to scale. I also go over the five aspects of a company that you need to support scalability and growth.

Part 2—Strengthen Your Company's Presence

Your company's *story*, *brand*, *values*, and *culture* are unlikely to create themselves magically or even organically. The best companies carefully create and orchestrate these four elements, playing them together for maximum impact, recognition, engagement, and inspiration. When done well, your story-brand-value-culture is a powerful way to communicate your company's intentions, authenticity, and goodwill.

Part 3—Hire, Empower, and Support Your Most Important Resources

It's more important to hire on P.h.D. traits than actual experience or skills; find out what to look for when hiring for P.h.D. Next, I'll go into what it takes to keep your employees for the long-term as the valuable assets that they are. It's simpler than you think (and it's not about the money). Trust me, your company benefits even more than the employees do. Also, learn how performance management makes it easier to communicate expectations and keep everyone working toward the same company-wide goal.

Part 4—Build a Sales Team, Calculate Sales Efficiency, and Sales' Secret Weapon

I'll help you in the all-important task of building a sales team and determining if you have an effective sales process. Plus, discover how creating *another* team can lead to stronger and happier Sales and Marketing employees.

Part 5—An Operational Plan for Short-Term Survival, Adaptability for the Long-Term

Stop spending your days putting out fires and get everyone focused on your most immediate goals as well as ones for the long-term. Also, what can

Blockbuster and Netflix teach you about adaptability? Look at the traits you need – personally and as a company – to stay in the public eye for 10, 20, or even 50 more years.

One More Thing Before We Start...

This is what I believe, and it hasn't steered me wrong yet:

#1 It all comes down to enjoying every minute of what you do.

#2 The key to leadership is enabling others to be the best they can be and supporting them along the way.

#3 The key to success is having *passion, hustle, and drive* in everything you do.

When you add 1, 2, and 3 together, there is no limit to how much you can grow yourself and your business!

Chapter 1 – Is It Time to Scale?

Before you begin to plan your scaling strategy, you first need to ask yourself, "Am I ready to scale?" But here's the rub… in order to answer *that* question, you must first answer other questions:

❖ Does your company have a consistent income?

❖ Is your company growing?

❖ Have you achieved some level of automation?

❖ Is your business model scalable?

These questions are relevant to all companies. By answering the questions truthfully, you will have a better idea on where you company currently stands and if it is ready to scale.

But before we get into the questions, I want to clarify what I mean by scaling. Simply stated, it means that your business has the potential to multiply revenue with minimal incremental cost.

"Ready to scale" is when you have a proven product and a proven business model that can expand to new geographies and markets. But the real goal is to increase revenue while still keeping operating costs the same or minimally higher. That's a *scalable* business. In contrast, if you are growing your revenue, but you're also increasing your operating costs, that's not scaling… that's just growth.

Therefore, in order to scale your company properly, you must figure out how you are going to increase revenue without a marked increase in operating costs. This is not an easy task. (If it were easy, everyone would be doing it.) Furthermore, it is different for every single business, so I can't tell you exactly how to go about it. But what I can provide are some basic principles for you to apply to your business.

Question 1: Does Your Company Have a Consistent Income?

If your month-to-month income is not at a consistent level, it's probably not yet time to scale. Instead, take the time to ramp up on marketing, leads, and sales. (Make sure you check out the sales-related Chapters 9 and 10 in this book.) You can always reassess your scalability potential in three to six months.

Even if you are consistently making a stable income every month, if you are still having money trouble, now is not a good time to scale. A financial advisor or a bookkeeper can review your financial statements, determine where your money is going, and help you find better ways to manage the cash.

Question 2: Is Your Company Growing?

If you have added employees but haven't seen any corresponding growth in new business or production, that's a problem. As your company grows in size, it must also bring in more revenue to pay those additional salaries and other expenses that come with hiring employees.

Stagnant growth could indicate two things:

❖ You are still performing the majority of tasks yourself.

❖ Your employees may not know what they're doing (to put it bluntly).

It may be necessary for you to delegate more tasks, hire outside help (consultants, freelancers, etc.), automate some tasks, or retrain your employees.

Speaking of training, you should also free yourself the constant "how do I" questions by putting into place policies and procedures for running your business. If you feel a sense of uncertainty or mistrust about handing over tasks to your employees, then you need to take a hard look at your policies and procedures. It's important to have documentation on how your business operates. Without it, new employees don't get trained properly, and existing employees don't consistently perform their jobs to your level of excellence. This can lead to workplace inefficiency, poor products and/or services, and eventually – chaos.

Question 3: Have You Achieved Some Level of Automation?

Although it's typical to work long hours for weeks at a time when you are first starting up a business, this isn't something that's viable over a long period of time. If you have been in business awhile and have employees, yet you are still working 12 or 14 hours days, you are at risk of burning out. Not only is this unhealthy for you, it's unhealthy for your business.

Look for repetitive and time-consuming tasks or business processes that can be automated with technology. Some examples of this include:

- ❖ *Collaboration tools*—Whether or not your team works in different parts of the country (or globe!), you'll spend less time searching through emails and folders if you use software that supports online communication and collaboration. *Examples:* Asana, Basecamp, and Slack

- ❖ *Social media management*—Software that helps you manage your social media accounts (Facebook, Twitter, Instagram, etc.) can save a lot of time. *Example:* Hootsuite, Zoho Social, Buffer, Sprout Social

- ❖ *Customer relationship management*—Since sales is the lifeblood of your company, it makes sense to invest in software that organizes and automates your lead generation process. Salesforce is one example, but if you don't need all those bells and whistles, there are more affordable apps. *Example:* Yetiforce

- ❖ *Human resources tasks*—Software can help streamline the hiring process, bring on new employees, and organize the training process. *Examples:* Namely and BambooHR

Although it does take time to implement and learn new software, you will reap the benefits many times over by lowering your frustration level and freeing up more of your time for business development.

Question 4: Is Your Business Model Scalable?

If your business needs more input in order to create more output, then it is going to be difficult to increase your income without also increasing your cost of doing business. A couple of examples of this is if you must hire more salespeople to generate more sales or hire more production workers to manufacture more items.

Of course, if the revenue you generate with each hire is so high that the resulting costs of salaries is negligible, hire away! However, it's more likely that you're like most companies; you must hire more employees to create more output, and it's going to be necessary for you to tweak your business model.

You need to find ways to add revenue without incurring costs that will always eat up your gains. Technology is one way to achieve this. Although the upfront cost of technology can be high, once it's in place, the cost goes down. You can use technology to offer more to your customers; you can also use it to reduce operating redundancies, thus reducing costs.

Another way to generate more income without incurring high cost is to add new distribution channels. If you sell a product or service to a very specific business or consumer niche, look into ways of widening the niche market, perhaps by adding a feature or value to the product or service.

Important Aspects of Scalability and Growth

Another way to assess if your company is ready to scale is to consider the following aspects of your business:

❖ Foundation

❖ Communication

❖ Future Mindset

❖ Strategy

❖ Marketplace Awareness

Foundation

Put time and energy into foundational systems that will support growth. This could range from a training program for new employees to purchasing financial software that automates invoicing and bill paying.

Wherever possible, look for ways to automate tasks so that you can focus on scaling your business. In addition, by standardizing and documenting your business processes, you free up employees for more creative and/or revenue-generating tasks.

Communication

As the CEO, COO or founder/co-founder of your company, you're the one who has grown it to its current state. You know your company's past and present, and you have a vision for its future.

However, in order to scale, it's important to provide the means for you and your employees to encourage and exchange ideas. The workday environment should be conductive to sharing ideas, meaning that ridiculing or ignoring ideas is not allowed. Be willing to work on developing an idea that may not seem viable at first.

Even if an idea doesn't work out, if you've taken the time to think through an idea, your employees will notice and appreciate this; they'll be more willing to share other ideas in the future… and one of those could be a strong revenue generator.

Future Mindset

What's typical of startups is to find the cheapest and fastest solution to a problem and keep moving. You may call it bootstrapping and pride yourself on it, but the downside is that it can lead to a bigger problem. Eventually, you could find yourself with inefficient processes and systems that work poorly together or are so intricate and "manual" that only you know how to run the business. Before scaling, you'll need to find those inefficiencies and replace them with something better, something that can help your company grow.

Ideally, you need to take the time to build in future capacity to handle increased workload. What you don't want to happen is to experience surprising growth that you're not prepared for. If that happens, you'll find yourself scrambling, hiring inappropriate employees who only add to expenses without increasing production or purchasing expensive equipment or software at a premium price.

Strategy

It's easy to get caught up in putting out the latest fires in your business, but if you want to scale your business, you must learn how to think strategically. This is what it means to work ON your business instead of IN your business.

You're going to have to set aside a block of time – preferably every day – to work on exactly how you plan to scale. You must also get comfortable delegating tasks, not only to your employees, but also to resources outside of your business, such as freelancers or companies that provide business services.

Marketplace Awareness

Along with thinking strategically, you need to have an awareness of where your business stands in the marketplace. Some people monitor their industry through networking and business events. Others prefer to read industry journals, blogs, and so forth. That's part of having marketplace awareness.

Another aspect is being able to recognize opportunities and threats. Looking for opportunities often requires you to think outside of your normal vendors and clients (i.e., outside the box). Identifying threats isn't just about your competition. It could mean new regulations or laws that could detrimentally affect your business.

Yet one more aspect of marketplace awareness is your brand. Before scaling, you should have done a lot of work on your brand, even beyond your logo, packaging, uniforms, and so forth. It should be a no-brainer for prospects and customers to distinguish between your brand and your competitors' brands.

Chapter Summary

We've touched on a lot of topics in this chapter, so I want to summarize them there:

Stabilize Your Income Stream

It's crucial that you have a strong flow of income from which to draw during your scaling activities. Automate or standardize marketing and sales activities so that you have a consistent income stream.

Communicate Clearly and Regularly

Communicate to your team and other employees about your company goals so that your new focus isn't a surprise to them. The more consistently and successfully you communicate the vision, the more likely it is that you will transfer your enthusiasm and interest in scaling to your employees (and the less likely it is that they will see this as just another corporate fad).

Find Ways to Automate

Find ways to eliminate redundancies, especially in production areas. As much as possible, remove yourself from day-to-day operating tasks so that you can focus on scaling and business development activities. Use technology to lower costs and/or add more features or value to your product/service.

Get your ducks in a row by evaluating all areas of your business. Remove inefficiencies and frustrations and make it easy to increase production without having to hire additional employees. Look for areas of your business that might create an operating bottleneck. This can often require adding technology in the form of equipment or software, but not always. Sometimes just adding or changing a step in your standard operating procedure can cut days off of getting your product or service to the customer.

Tweak Your Business Model

Take a hard look at your business model and decide if it's possible to tweak it in such a way that you can increase revenue without incurring the additional cost of doing business.

Practice Thinking Strategically

Besides thinking more about how your business operates, setting aside a block of time to think and develop business ideas gets you in the habit of thinking strategically. Remember, this is working *on* your business instead of always working *in* it.

To generate ideas, examine all aspects of your industry, from competitors to customers to vendors. Try not to censor ideas that pop into your head, as this can stifle creativity. Give all new ideas, especially those volunteered by your employees, the respect they deserve.

What new behavior or habit has most improved your life?

MIKITA MIKADO

Meditation. Learning to meditate helped me to get a tool to cool off and reset the way I think about problems and opportunities.

SAMAR BIRWADKER

Given that speed and flexibility are a startup's biggest assets, my daily schedule is generally unpredictable and having too much process can actually end up being counter-productive. Because of this, I try to carve out two hours every day as power-hours – no matter what time of day, those two hours are precious and must happen. It helps me get stuff done quickly without distractions and balance the urgent with the strategic.

KYLE PORTER

Grounding as a child of God. I want to never put my security in something that can be taken away from me.

Chapter 2 – It's All About the Story!

Maybe the idea of telling the story of your business seems silly or self-centered to you. *Who wants to know all that stuff?* you're thinking.

However, there are several reasons why people do want to hear your story. There is also ample evidence that proves a company with an interesting story can distinguish itself from its competitors and gain more market share.

Once you understand the power of storytelling and how it ties into your company's brand, I believe you'll agree with me that stories not only snag a prospect's attention, they also sway them over to your side by supporting your company's authenticity, originality, and uniqueness.

Even if you are one of those already skilled at entrancing listeners or readers with the tale of how your company was born, I'd like you to keep reading. I believe you'll pick up some tips on how to enhance and extend your storytelling skills.

What We Mean by Story

The kind of stories I'd like you to think about have to do with how your company got started, where it got its name, the various struggles it has faced, and so forth. Another type of story to consider is your employees' and customers' stories (more on that later).

If you are still puzzled by what is meant by your company's story, go to the Starbucks' website and read its story. Although it's comprised of just a few hundred words, it conveys a lot of information:

❖ How the company got started

❖ Where the company got its name

❖ The company's original niche market

❖ How the company pivoted to change its focus

One warning… the company stories you'll read online, especially for mega corporations like Google, Apple, Amazon, and so forth, have been carefully crafted and polished. Don't get discouraged if your initial efforts aren't similar to these pieces. What's important right now is to get your story down in writing. The polishing and primping comes later.

Why Use a Story

So why all the attention to "the story?" Let me give you just a few reasons why your company's story carries so much weight:

❖ Everyone understands stories.

❖ Your company's story distinguishes you from the crowd.

❖ Stories are more interesting and easily remembered than facts.

In fact, your story can serve as the backbone of your brand. You can use the ideas, theme, or emotions suggested by your story to help craft your brand image, your core values, and even your company culture. (More on those topics in later chapters.)

Everyone Understands Stories

By "everyone" I mean everyone on this planet. Stories are understood across the globe and are an integral part of every culture. Stories have been used for thousands of years to communicate a culture's history, ideas, and lessons.

Even before stories were written down, they were communicated verbally around the nightly fire or hearth. Even after stories were written down, society had a special name for storytellers – *bards*. In a time before radio, television, and computers, the bard or local storyteller was the main source of entertainment in most societies.

Besides imparting important information about society's rules and other life lessons, stories were popular because they evoked emotions. Nowadays, the "best" stories go on the *New York Times* Bestseller List, but back then, the best stories were repeated from generation to generation.

Although our intellectual side takes a deep interest in facts and other types of concrete information, stories – because they have their claws in our emotions – speak to us on a deep, intuitive level. We might claim we make decisions based on "the facts," but the *real* fact is… we make decisions based on our emotions. And since stories have the power to evoke emotion, we'd be foolish to ignore its potential advantage in applying it to our businesses.

Stories are More Interesting and Easily Remembered Than Facts

Besides evoking emotion in us, stories are simply more interesting than numbers, statistics, benefits, and features. Although that information *is* important to provide to your prospects and customers, it's not going to be as easy to remember as your story.

With so much easy access to information over the past decade, consumers have gotten smarter in how they approach their purchases. Nowadays, a serious buyer completes a large part of research into your product/service before they contact you. Your story can make a difference between you and your competitors.

Stories Distinguish You from the Crowd and Enhance Your Brand

When you think about how much information we modern consumers are exposed to on a daily basis, it's a wonder our heads don't explode. Nowadays, the average consumer is overwhelmed by information, especially of the marketing variety. They have learned to ignore advertising and tune out marketing messages. Consumers can click to delete an email or unsubscribe. They can record their television shows and fast-forward through commercials.

There is research that strongly supports the competitive advantage of companies with a compelling story and legacy. In addition, a story is the best medium for prospects and customers to understand what your business is all about. Stories help humanize a business.

When you weave your company's story into your overall marketing strategy, it is much more likely that you will reap the benefits of loyalty and affection from your customers. Who knows? Some stories have become legend – like the Bill Gates story of starting up Microsoft in his garage or King Arthur's round table. One day your company may be enshrined there along with them.

What Can Go Into a Story

If you read novels or watch movies, you might wonder how a business and a story can even share the same room together. To you a story might need to have light sabers, car chases, comedy, or a happily-ever-after romance. However, there are many different kinds of stories. In fact, the following is a type of story:

The XYZ, LLC was founded in 1999 in Nashville, Tennessee. By the end of 2001, the company had grown to 15 employees and was generating a revenue of $1.5 million per year.

The problem is, it's rather dull, isn't it? It's chock full of dates, dollars, and other facts, although this might be appropriate for an investment prospectus or appeal to someone on an intellectual level.

The most interesting stories all have common elements (more on that later), but in general, humans most appreciate a story that affects their emotions; fear, excitement, love, hate, and sympathy are just a handful of the range of human emotion.

Have you ever heard the German word *schadenfreude*? It literally means "harm-joy," and it's a cultural expression for our fascination and pleasure in hearing about others' misfortune, trials, and trouble. This may seem rather morbid and unkind to you, but it is just a fact of human nature for all but the saintliest of humans.

I bring up *schadenfreude* because I think it's important for you to understand that people like to read about others' problems and tribulations. They may empathize with it or they may revel in it, but the point is that *it grabs their attention*.

Understanding this fact of human nature is one way to make a reader pause. Even if they don't feel the actual naughty pleasure of *schadenfreude*, it's highly likely that they will want to stick around to hear how it all turns out.

Besides using *schadenfreude* to your advantage, look for other emotions – both positive and negative – that will help people feel a connection. Some likely emotions are sympathy, amusement, inspiration, and intrigue. Negative emotions are a bit more difficult to use, but are still powerful, such as outrage, anger, sorrow, and anxiety, all of which can motivate a person to act or respond in some way.

Although it's perfectly acceptable to mention winning a battle (figuratively speaking) and the ongoing success of one's company, in general it's not going to be as interesting to others unless you can communicate the difficulties that were hidden like landmines along the way.

To recap, covering your struggles, hardships, and setbacks is good. Bragging about market share and the easy uphill climb to success – not so good.

Questions to Get Started

To help get your creative juices flowing as you write out your company's story, try answering some questions about your beginnings:

❖ How did you get the idea to start your business?

❖ How did your company get its name?

❖ Has your hometown, your family, or your friends provided the inspiration for your business?

❖ What are you passionate about?

❖ What was the worst thing that happened to you when you were building your business?

❖ Are you still providing the original product/service that you started out with? Why or why not?

❖ Did you get a "big break" (or even an "aha!" moment) that helped skyrocket your business?

❖ Where is your product made?

❖ Why do employees like working for your company?

If You're Stuck or Lose Inspiration

If you find it difficult to get started or lose your inspiration, you can get input from friends, family, and co-workers who were there in the beginning. It may surprise (and inspire) you to hear your company's story from another person's point of view.

Another way to get the creative juices flowing is to read other company's stories. Read each story one time, then go back through it and pick out the important elements. This is actually how many authors have learned how to tell a short story or write a novel... by looking at what has worked (i.e., the works of successfully published authors). A more technical term for it is *reverse engineering*. If you want me to read your story and give you pointers, feel free to contact me.

Communicate a Story with the Five Cs

In the beginning, while you're working on the first draft of your company's story, it's important to not self-edit or critique as you write. Later on, you can work on honing it, choosing your words more carefully, and layering the story with the tips and techniques mentioned in this section.

To begin, jot down the major points of your story (using the questions in the previous section to get started). You can use the "five Cs" of storytelling to make sure you have included the most important elements:

❖ Circumstances

❖ Curiosity

❖ Characters

❖ Conversation

❖ Conflict

Circumstances

The circumstances have to do with setting the stage, letting the reader know what's going on in the story. This includes the where and when (and perhaps the why) of the story. This information gives the reader the information necessary to interpret the story. For example, San Francisco has quite a different ambiance than New York City, just like the 1960s had a different vibe than the 1990s.

Curiosity

If you can resist the desire to give the reader (or listener) all of the information immediately, you can create the desire in them to want to learn more. Curiosity can also be stimulated by unusual circumstances, like leaving your well-furnished condo to live for 12 weeks in an old school bus or using your French bulldog as a company mascot. Another technique is to *not* explain a person's actions in the story until later. You can enhance a person's curiosity by not giving them all of the information in the first paragraph… by delivering it in small chunks throughout your story. Cultivating curiosity can be one of the more difficult techniques to master, but you'll get better with practice.

Characters

Every story has its actors or characters. What's important here is to keep everyone human and believable. Think of it this way… isn't it rather dull to visit a company's website and see stock photos of perfect models posing as office workers or customers? Instead, it's much more interesting to see photos of real people. It's just more authentic. Keep this in mind when telling your story; there is no Superman in real life.

Conversation

Because we are human, we are sociable, and because we are sociable, we like to talk and text… in other words, have conversations. How many times has your curiosity been piqued by a friend saying, "Guess what so-and-so said?" or by overhearing a fragment of conversation in a public place? Try to find a way to work conversation into your story because it helps to break up longer paragraphs and can help humanize your "characters."

Conflict

I saved the best for last. Conflict in any form is of interest to humans. When telling your company's story, you can use two types of conflict, internal and external:

Internal conflict is related to characters' emotions, thoughts, and motivations.

External conflict has to do with circumstances (usually) out of our control, like the bank calling in the loan or the fire that destroyed all of your equipment.

Relaying the conflict also includes the resolution or solution of the problem. This doesn't mean that everything has to wrap up as neatly as a professionally wrapped gift, but don't leave the reader hanging, wondering what the current state of your company is.

Don't Forget Customer and Employee Stories

I mentioned earlier in this chapter that you can also talk to your employees if you're stuck in writing your company story or if you need some inspiration. I wanted to follow up on that and talk about employees' stories and customers' stories.

An employee's story is especially appealing if your company has in some way made an impact on that employee or changed that person's life. As an example, think of companies that sell weight loss products; it's quite common for someone to try the product, lose weight and begin living a healthier lifestyle, and then become an employee or affiliate of that company.

Publishing customers' stories as part of your company's marketing collateral is quite common; I'm sure you've heard of *case studies* (also called *success stories*) and their mini-versions, *testimonials*. However, case studies and the like have traditionally been full of facts and figures, and their purpose has been to demonstrate some improvement of the customer's situation or elimination of a problem thanks to the company's product or service. Instead of using the traditional approach, if you decide to write a customer success story, try to loosen it up a bit more to include the five Cs mentioned in the previous section.

Chapter Summary

Let's briefly go over this chapter's information:

Why Your Company's Story Is Important

Stories have been around for so long that they're practically woven into the human DNA (but don't quote me on that bit of scientific speculation). They appeal to people because of the emotion they evoke and their ability to stimulate our curiosity.

The Benefits of Sharing Your Story

There is research that suggests a company with a strong story and legacy has a competitive advantage. Use your company's story to grab people's attention in a world already saturated with "information." Once you have their attention, the story also does the hard work of introducing yourself to your customers, conveying your company's history, and supporting your brand. In the next chapter, I'll go into more detail on how to build your brand.

Important Story Elements

While there are many different types of stories, remember to keep the numbers, dollar amounts, and statistics to a minimum. Also, watch out for unrestrained bragging of your multiple successes. People are more interested in hearing about the problems you've faced and how you've surmounted them. Remember the German word *schadenfreude*!

Even More Important Story Elements: The Five Cs

Don't forget that your story needs to have the important elements of circumstance, curiosity, characters, conversation, and more important of all… conflict! If you can provide a good balance of these in your storytelling, then it's likely that thousands will read your story and share it with others.

Who is one person that has greatly influenced your life and your growth?

MIKITA MIKADO

One person I'd mention is the guy I rented a room from the first time I got to US. His name is Daryl, and he is an old Japanese guy. My first two years here were rough. I had to work 16-hour work days making a minimum wage. Daryl was the person who constantly encouraged me to keep going and keep fighting. He was the person who constantly told me, "Don't worry. It is hard now, but eventually you're going to make it." And that is exactly what I needed back then.

SCOTT LEESE

My dad is one of the most successful soccer coaches in Northern CA and a professor for 40 years. Seeing the dedication, commitment, excellence, and lifelong learning he applied to his disciplines is too valuable to even measure.

RICHARD HARRIS

I will go out on a limb here and get very personal, quickly. It's my psychologist. In 2000/2001 I was a single male living in San Francisco but hating it. I had low self-esteem, depression, and had no work-life balance.

One day I woke up and physically could not get out of bed. I was weeping uncontrollably. Everything should have been amazing, but for me it was not. So, I called my mom to get some advice. Her first piece of advice was to move home, back to Georgia. I explained that was not an option. If I did that, then "The City" would have won. It would have beat me. I was not willing to do that, no matter how bad I was feeling.

She called some friends and found someone who happened to be the right person for me. My therapist helped me find myself, discover who I truly needed to be at that time and what I wanted to become in the future.

I've learned that when you have big life changes, it's good to have someone to talk with about the things that bother you. Yes, you can do it with friends and family members, but if you can find a true mentor, a life coach, or a shrink, there is nothing better than having someone help you check yourself from time to time and help you remember your core.

I'll also say that I'm fortunate because not everyone has the ability to find a therapist, much less a great one for themselves. My advice here is find someone you can trust who will listen, and they will call you out on your own bullshit.

BOB MARSH

Josh Linkner, who was the founder and CEO of ePrize, which was my third job about five years after graduating from college. I joined ePrize as a salesperson about a year after the company started, and I really struggled for a good year. But Josh saw something in me and kept me around. I knew I had the ability, and for some reason so did he.

The company was struggling, and we went from 15 - 20 salespeople down to about four, so Josh putting his cards on me was quite a statement. Eventually it clicked for me, and I really flourished, becoming one of the company's top sellers, moved into sales management, and eventually executive leadership.

Along the way, Josh hired other great people, whom I learned a ton from, and I continued to learn from observing his leadership as well. After ePrize was sold successfully to a private equity firm in 2012, I used that experience to found LevelEleven, which was creating software to run all the things I learned in my years as a seller and manager. Josh ran the VC firm that backed our initial investment and has continued to be a mentor and a great friend. Plus, he's just fun to hang out with!

SAMAR BIRWADKER

Muhammad Ali

KYLE PORTER

My wife, April, no doubt. She shares in the highs and lows and never stops believing.

Chapter 3 – Build Your Brand

A brand is much more than an attractive logo, and branding is like developing the reputation you want your business to have. This chapter covers most of what you need to consider when developing a brand and how to go about disseminating your brand once it's fully developed.

Branding is my special arena of knowledge, and I've written much more on this topic in an eBook, *The "B" Word: Becoming Foolishly Bold in Creating the Ultimate Brand.* Check it out for the full scoop on brands and branding, including real-life examples from companies like Google, Monster Energy, and Nike.

Why Your Brand – and Branding – Is Important

One of the reasons why branding is so important is found in human nature. Given the choice between two products that are exactly the same (including the price), how does a person choose between them? Simple… that person will choose the product that he or she recognizes as a "better brand."

For this reason, it's crucial for you to take charge of branding by building the image you want in the minds of your customers. This image must be strong enough that your brand actually becomes part of their lives.

What's in a Brand?

Think of your favorite company.

You probably first think of its products or services. You remember past experiences with the product or service and perhaps anticipate future experiences. In short, thoughts of the company conjure up good feelings.

If you had to try to explain your overall experiences with the company, depending on the product or service, you might use words like: fun, easy, hilarious, simple, delicious… you get the idea. These words describe more than just the product or service. They are part of the company's brand.

A company's brand is *also* about:

❖ How your customers perceive the company

❖ How the company communicates with customers

❖ What the company's customers say about it

❖ Where the company came from (*a.k.a.* your company's story)

❖ Anything else? Well… yes. There's that intangible aspect best described as "attitude" or "personality." Added in to this mix is your company's products (or services), and a "look and feel" (name, logo, etc.).

What Is Branding?

Branding is the act of defining your brand's identity, but it's also the act of disseminating it (spreading the word). With these two steps, you are building your company's platform. You can also think of it as your company's foundation or your company's image.

You are already familiar with *broad-scope branding* in the form of TV commercials or online Facebook advertisements. However, the branding you want for your new business is *niche focus*, also referred to as *narrow branding*.

Niche focus branding is about connecting with your audience in a way that shows you can help them solve a problem, improve their situation, or meet their needs. It's customer-focused in that you take the spotlight off your company and aim it at your target audience. Because it is so customer-oriented, niche focus is closely allied with social media marketing.

Great Branding Takes Deliberation and Thought

The less tangible aspects of branding mentioned earlier can seem a bit difficult to nail down but nail them down you must. Fortunately, you've already done some of the mental work by writing out your company's story. (If you skipped the last chapter, go back and read it now!)

Here are some points to consideration when branding your business:

❖ Study the competition

❖ Use your company's story as a launching pad

❖ Consider the customers' problems

❖ Establish principles and values

❖ Figure out what "above and beyond" means

❖ Polish it off with the perfect name and logo

Study the Competition

Become very familiar with other brands in your industry so that you know how to differentiate your business. Pin down exactly how your business is different from the competition. If you can't see a difference, that's definitely something you need to work on!

Later in this section, there are some helpful suggestions in differentiating yourself via authenticity and going above and beyond. And of course, your company's story is completely unique.

Use Your Company's Story as a Launching Pad

If you are having trouble seeing anything in your company's story that can be associated with its brand, try getting help from a third party. This could be someone who knows you or your business very well but has a different way of thinking than you do. Or it could be someone who is not very familiar with your or your business, yet is known for being intuitive, empathic, or creative. Sometimes, it takes a near stranger to point out something that is right in front of our face!

Consider the Customers' Problems

Refresh your accumulated knowledge and details about your average customer or target audience. Using the information, you already have about your average customer, think about their problems. How does your product or service help solve these problems? What are the benefits of using your product or service? How is this solution different from your competitors?

Establish Principles and Values

Nowadays, consumers aren't as willing to fork over their hard-earned cash to nameless corporations. They expect a company to exhibit the characteristics that reflect the best of humanity, such as kindness, thoughtfulness, and integrity. Most people also prefer to give their money to a company that will give back to and care about the community.

This isn't meant to encourage you to adopt a false front of compassion or become boastful about how much money your company donated to charity. For one, anything that isn't truthful or genuine about your company will be instantly detected by modern consumers' excellent phony detectors. More importantly, it's better to humbly represent what you stand for because that is what is appreciated by today's discerning customers – authenticity.

Authenticity is born out of a company's internal values and intentions. An authentic company practices what it preaches and holds true to its guiding principles. You can express your company's authenticity with:

- ❖ *Story*—Your story has to power to evoke an audience's emotions. And if there's anything that feels authentic, it's emotions (*a.k.a.* feelings). The previous chapter discusses all the important aspects of your company's story.

- ❖ *Originality*—You're not a copycat, and you're not riding anyone else's coattails to success.

- ❖ *Real value*—Your product or service is something that your customers can't live without or don't want to do without.

- ❖ *Core values*—Summarize your company's principles or guiding ideas, such as honesty, efficiency, high standards, environmental concern, and so forth. I'll discuss this topic in-depth in the next chapter.

Figure Out What "Above and Beyond" Means

One surefire way to set yourself apart from the competition is to understand the difference between just satisfying your customers and going beyond their expectations. Even if your most successful competitor already claims to be going "above and beyond" for the customer, you can find a way to top that. That's the beauty of going above and beyond.

I'm not saying it's easy to figure out, and it will be different for every industry or specialized market. However, you have already done a large part of the brain-work in defining how you solve your customers' problems. Now you just need to turn up the dial. Some examples can be lifetime warranties, deep discounts to special customers, customizing items, or special-order items.

Polish It Off with the Perfect Name and Logo

Now that you have worked on getting the less tangible concepts of your brand on paper (or the screen), it should be easier to work on the more concrete aspects, such as the name and logo.

Pages and pages have been written on this topic. I won't even try to repeat that here, but I do have some advice before you work on these aspects of your brand.

Company Name

Your company name should be unique and timeless. (Easier said than done, right?) On top of that, you should try to have a company name that is descriptive or suggestive of your company's product or service.

Besides being happy with the way your company name looks, you need to make sure it's easy to pronounce and spell. It's better to have a short-and-sweet name than a longer one. Don't forget to check if it has a different meaning or connotation in another language.

Another significant factor to consider is the domain name (website address) you can obtain. If the domain name you want isn't available, you may be able to purchase it from its current owner.

Logo

Your company logo is important, but you don't want to overthink it, or you might end up with a logo that is overly complicated. But it's also not the time to play it safe, or your logo will be uninteresting and easily forgettable.

Like your company name, the logo should be unique and feel timeless. It should also take into consideration the nature of your business and target audience. (Think of the Baby Einstein logo versus the BMW logo.)

Color will obviously come into play here. It's been well researched that colors can summon emotional responses from people. Use that knowledge to select a color scheme that reflects your brand's overall message. Below is a list of colors and the general emotions they evoke:

- ❖ **Red**—Passion, excitement, boldness

- ❖ **Orange**—Retro, friendliness, warmth

- ❖ **Yellow**—Cheerfulness, freshness, spring and summer

- ❖ **Green**—Health and wellness, trustworthiness, natural and earthy

- ❖ **Blue**—Trust, smart, stability, authority, soothing

- ❖ **Purple**—Eclectic, fun, feminine, stylish

- ❖ **Brown**—Warm, professional, retro

Branding in Action

Once you nail down these aspects as part of your brand, your next step it to consistently communicate it while interacting with your customers. That interaction can be face-to-face, by telephone or print, or via email, Twitter, Facebook, or other social media.

Engage Your Audience

As mentioned earlier in the chapter, one of the hallmarks of niche focus branding is that its attention is firmly aimed at the customer. Consumers are fed up with being "sold to" and "talked at" by advertisers and marketers. Instead, they want to be able to connect with their favorite brands, either because it's already a part of their lives or because they have something important they want you to know.

When starting and maintaining conversations with your customers, remember that it isn't about marketing. Instead, your intent should be to engage people. Here are some "Do's" and "Don'ts" in regard to communicating your brand:

DO	DON'T
Engage in actual conversation with fans, prospects, customers, supporters, and followers.	Spout nothing but ads or links to your products.
Share and promote others.	Bash competitors for any reason – even if they deserve it.
Answer questions or concerns, particularly if they are about your products or touch on something your product or service can help with.	Blatantly promote yourself for no reason at all.

Although the above tips are based on social media marketing "rules," they apply perfectly here. Neither social media or branding is the time for shameless self-promotion.

One of the ways to enter a conversation gracefully is to help solve a problem. You can offer empathy and, if appropriate, make suggestions that include your products.

You can also ask questions to learn more about your customers and how they use your products or services. This also opens up the opportunity to ask them about their actual needs.

Another part of branding is to become an expert in your industry or niche. When you hold that trusted position, your brand is naturally perceived as the best choice.

One way to open up communication *and* position you and your company as an expert is through blogging. Through a blog, you can share stories and real conversations with customers, news and background about your industry, and other tidbits of information.

If you can't bring yourself to blog on a regular basis (consistency is important), you can still distribute information via articles and newsletters (whether hard copy or electronic). Offer your advice or information freely, without expecting anything in return.

Keep in Touch

Once you have defined your brand and are actively engaged in branding, there's just one thing left to do... get better at it! If you have established yourself as an expert in your field, you need to remain innovative and original so that you can stay one step ahead of your competition.

This may sound like "one more thing to do" on top of your other business responsibilities, but it doesn't have to be elaborate or expensive:

- ❖ Read the most popular blogs in your industry or those related to your industry.

- ❖ Subscribe to news and publications about your industry.

- ❖ Communicate frequently with your customers and employees (preferably one-on-one) and ask them about their experiences with your service or product. Transform these related experiences into stories and of course – share them!

- ❖ Take some creative time alone every day or every week to jot down ideas and develop them into branding action plans. (If you recall, I mentioned this in Chapter 1 in regard to thinking strategically and working *on* your business instead of just *in* your business.)

By keeping up-to-date on the latest tools, materials, and concepts in your industry, you'll do more than just stay ahead of the competition. You'll also discover new and novel ways to meet the needs of your customers – maybe even before they've identified it as a "need" themselves!

Consider How to Reach Out to Your Target Audience

Consider your target audience. What is the best way to reach them? If they're the Greatest Generation, Twitter probably isn't the best answer here. But that might work for Millennials. You also need to consider the potential cost of reaching out to your audience.

It can help to put yourself in their shoes and consider how you would like to be approached. Will it feel intrusive to them? Are there any privacy concerns?

Stay Calm and Keep Branding

If branding seems overwhelming, please remain calm. Branding isn't accomplished in a day, a week, or even months. It's based on taking small steps every day. If you are consistent, over time you'll see the momentum behind your brand built and take on a life of its own.

Chapter Summary

In this chapter, I've gone over what makes up a brand and the various ways you can engage in branding. Although the concept for a brand may just pop into your head one day, the overall development and implementation of a brand requires some consideration and deliberation.

Before working on your brand or developing it further, make sure you clearly understand your customer and the competition. You should have also developed your company's story (Chapter 2). Coming up with a company name and logo will be easier if you've accomplished these tasks.

Of course, communicating your brand is where you start to see it all pay off. Remember, though, that it's not all about you. You're attempting to connect with people and have conversations with real and soon-to-be customers. You'll have a lot more credibility if you prove that you can apply your product knowledge to help them solve a problem (even if you don't directly gain from it).

Keeping in touch via a blog is great, but I don't recommend doing one if you think it will be torture for you. There are other ways to keep your brand not too far out-of-mind with your customers, like the most popular social media sites. The social media sites you select depend on which ones your customers use most frequently.

Above all, keep working at it, even if at first you see lackluster results. It can take time to build up a reputation and a brand, and it's better to go slowly anyway so that you can make minor adjustments along the way.

Do you have a favorite failure that helped set the stage for success that you would be open to share?

MIKITA MIKADO

I had a really good employee who quit PandaDoc but gave me a fantastic exit feedback. Back then I loved getting in the weeds whenever I've seen something not working, especially if getting in the weeds meant doing something technically challenging. That messed up work, strategy, and plans of other employees at PandaDoc. I hated to lose the guy, and I took his feedback to heart. I wouldn't say I'm not guilty of jumping in the weeds today, but I'm definitely aware of the issue and try to get out whenever I notice it.

SCOTT LEESE

My first time ever being considered for a sales manager role, I got passed over for somebody with more tenure, despite clearly being the better candidate. I thought about leaving the company, but I didn't. I stayed and decided I would make it impossible for them not to promote me, and I broke my own sales record by 3x. That person was fired within months, and I took over. Best thing I did was stick it out instead of bail.

BOB MARSH

Could we write another book just on this topic? I'm only half kidding – we all learn the most from our failures, and it's vital to use those to fuel your future performance.

While I can't point to any single thing, I can say that one thing I've continued to get much better at is trusting my gut, especially as it relates to hiring. Over time I've gained a good sense of people who I think will fit within our organization or that I can work well with if they're going to report directly to me.

So, the past failure would be not listening to – or really not trusting – my instincts when it comes to hiring people. Sometimes what seems perfectly rationale just doesn't feel right, and you must trust that feeling.

SAMAR BIRWADKER

In 2011, I had a pivotal culture fit experience. I had left a company that I enjoyed working at to go to greener pastures at a competitor that many would kill to work for. While I had done my due-diligence prior to accepting this offer, it took me a mere two days to realize it was a complete cultural misfit for me. For six months, I tried to focus on the positives and to tough it out, while trying to figure out why nobody had figured out a way to stop this from happening. After all it's a painful (and costly) problem for both the employee AND employer.

This set me thinking. The explosion of information in the last 5 - 10 years has brought unprecedented transparency in our lives, the benefit of which remains "top down." A potential employer can find out everything about an employee being evaluated – background checks, social media investigation, exhaustive interviews, personality tests, you name it. But what about the little guy? The job seeker still has no sources of credible information in evaluating what he/she is walking into – there is no bottom-up transparency!

Ultimately, this experience gave rise to the idea of Good&Co – a platform that allows users to understand their strengths, get insights about their working relationships and fit with their current job as well as the opportunity to identify jobs and teams that might be a better fit with not just their skills, but their personality, beliefs, and ambitions.

KYLE PORTER

Cease and desist letters. They test the character and resolve of my mission.

Chapter 4 – Establish Your Core Values

It's now time to better describe your company's intentions and reason for being. These are commonly referred to as your company's "core values." You can also think of your core values as the brand's character and what the company stands for.

In Chapters 2 and 3, I discussed the importance of your company having a story as well as a brand. You won't be surprised to know that the story and brand need to agree with your core values. For that reason, you might want to go back and skim over the past two chapters.

Just so you're thinking a bit ahead, you should also know that your company's core values form the basis of the workplace culture. But there will be more on that in the next chapter!

In this chapter, I'll discuss how to define core values that actually mean something to you and your employees.

Why Core Values Are Important

Core values help define the standards of behavior at a business so that it can keep itself on the right path. It's like having a compass or a guide. In many ways, it can make important decisions easier because you can first ask yourself, "Does this align with our organization's values?" This applies at the strategic level all the way down to day-to-day decisions.

One of the ways that core values can help you make better decisions is in hiring new employees. Job candidates might not list their core values on their resume (if only it were that easy), but it's certainly possible to determine after a few conversations if a person's values agree with your own.

Employees who work for a company that unswervingly communicates its core values are much more likely to feel in tune with other employees and the company at large. The core values, introduced when onboarding a new employee and visible on a daily basis, can help employees make better decisions and influence their behavior at work.

Sharing your company's core values with customers can positively influence them if your values align with theirs. Did you know that on a company website the About page is one of the four most visited sections?

As our society has become more sophisticated about making buying choices, it's not enough to just match the lowest price of your competitor. The internet has expanded the consumers' buying horizon and defining your core values helps to set you apart in a crowded marketplace.

What I Mean by Core Values

If you're still trying to understand what it means for a company to have core values, think about your own values, which can be determined with questions like these:

❖ What's important to you?

❖ What helps to guide you when you face a difficult situation?

❖ What are you proud of?

Just as your own values are different for everyone, a company's core values should be as unique to it as human fingerprints. The core values are a reflection of the company's identity, capturing the essence of the organization.

Just so I'm really clear, let me also define what core values are *not*:

❖ They are not values you *wish* your company had.

❖ They are not values that you *hope* to develop someday.

❖ They are not generic words that describe the minimum standards expected of all businesses (i.e., honesty, integrity).

One of the most important reasons for establishing strong, unique core values is that they will provide a blueprint for how your company will be run and how it will interact with employees and customers.

How to Define Your Company's Core Values

I hope you have a better understanding of what a company's core values mean to it as an organization, to its employees, and its customers. Defining your core values is a big step because you will share them with everyone and, in fact, think about or deal with them in some manner every workday.

It's Time to Make a Decision

You might still be feeling uncertain about this, and that's understandable. Maybe you don't believe core values have anything to do with your business. Perhaps you don't think they will add anything of worth to your organization.

If this is the case, you should set aside the idea of defining your core values (though I do encourage you to revisit the idea in about six months). I'm telling you this because unless you can wholeheartedly support and promote your company's core values, they really won't have any value.

In fact, implementing core values that you merely rubber-stamp into existence or core values that you drop the moment things get hectic will do more harm than good to your business. You risk losing your employees' respect, undermining your company leaders, and distancing your customers. Both employees and customers are very good at sniffing out pretenders and phonies. If you're not going to walk the talk with these core values, your company's reputation is actually better without them.

How to Define Your Company's Core Values

First, I'll go over the general steps for brainstorming and formally defining your organization's core values. After that, I have several recommendations that might help you during the process.

Remember, there is no one "right way" to define company values, just guidelines and recommendations. If your first attempt to put your core values down in black and white isn't successful, chalk it up to experience, and try again in a few days, weeks, or even months. I've found that approach to be very helpful when I'm trying to get something out of my head and onto paper, whether it's an idea, report, plan, or poem. (Just kidding... I don't write poetry.)

Here we go...

❖ *Who should be involved?* You and the core group of leaders in your business.

❖ *Where should we work on this?* Off-site, somewhere quiet and free from interruptions.

❖ *How do we get started?* Transition from your office location to the off-site location by taking a walk or some other activity that helps everyone relax and clear their minds.

Session 1—Brainstorming

1. Throw out an idea and discuss it.

2. If the group believes the suggestion has value, write it down.

3. Repeat this process until you wind up with a good number of ideas.

4. Take a break.

Session 2—Elimination Round

1. After a break, review what you have written down and eliminate any obvious ones that don't have support from the group. You may find that even though a core value doesn't resonate with you, it has a related concept that could branch off to a new idea.

2. Attempt to whittle down the list until you have what you believe are a rough set of core values.

3. Take another break.

Session 3—Fine-Tuning

1. Review this rough set of core values and discuss each one to fine-tune it. What you are trying to do here is be as specific as possible and eliminate any overlap or redundancies.

2. Save the list and set it aside for one week.

3. Meet again and go over each core value. With the passage of time, some new thoughts may have come up that need to be discussed or you might see a problem with one or more items.

Some Questions to Get the Creative Juices Flowing

Questions for brainstorming

- ❖ What's important to us?

- ❖ What do we like about this company?

- ❖ What part of the company are we particularly proud of?

- ❖ What do we believe are the values of our most treasured employee?

- ❖ What words or phrases do we relate to?

- ❖ What was the original idea that started this company?

- ❖ What is the "glue" that has held this company together?

- ❖ What words or phrases will help us to work through difficult situations or decisions?

Questions for eliminating

- ❖ Which one of these core values absolutely cannot be removed?

- ❖ What is more important: "delivering on deadline" or "delivering quality work?"

- ❖ What would cause us to tell a customer "no" or turn away a prospect?

- ❖ When is it okay to ask employees to sacrifice family time for work?

- ❖ What is more important: rapid expansion or slow, steady growth?

Questions for refining

- ❖ Does this core value fit in with our short- and long-term goals?

❖ Is this a core value we can believe in and support for the next three years? How about the next three years after that?

❖ Is it possible to hire people based on these core values?

❖ Would we be willing to let an employee go if they couldn't support these core values?

❖ Are these core values going to work for each area of the company? Operations? Product Development? Sales? Accounting?

Core Values Aren't Built by Mass Consensus

Although it might seem like a good idea to have input from everyone in the company about what they think the company's core values are, this isn't going to work. Here are a few reasons why:

❖ Not all of the people employed at your company actually belong there.

❖ It gives the false impression that everyone's input will be given equal weight or that the core values are to be decided on as a company.

❖ Depending on the size of your company, you may receive so much input that the process becomes overwhelming or frustrating.

If the idea of not including everyone at your company bothers you, think about it this way… you don't invite everyone to give input on the business's strategic plan, do you? You don't let them all give their opinion on the yearly budget, do you? Then why would you include them all in defining your company's most important values?

You might have such a small company that you don't have enough leaders and founders for brainstorming and discussion. In that case, you can include a few key employees in the process. Organizations larger than this that still want to include employee feedback can designate a few liaisons to solicit feedback or vet ideas before passing them on to the decision-making group.

Mine Values from Strife

One of the brainstorming questions I included up above is: *What words or phrases will help us to work through difficult situations or decisions?*

To help discover your company's core values, you might find it helpful to examine some of the most challenging situations your company has faced. How did you respond as a company or as a team? What values were the basis for the decisions you made?

If you can't think of a trying situation, then you need to be careful about finalizing your core values. You don't want to define your company around values that are only appropriate when things are going well. Remember that the core values can be used as a framework to guide future decisions. Make sure they can bear the weight of any turbulent times ahead!

Keep Core Values in the Forefront

It's one thing for a company to say that it "lives its values," but it's quite another to actually do it. Maybe this is so difficult to do because of the transition from the "talk" to the "walk." Obviously, every company is going to find a different way to work their core values into their day-to-day activities and behavior, but I have several recommendations that can help.

Roll Out and Training of the Core Values

When you are ready to introduce the company's core values to all of your employees, write up a plan for how this will take place. This is something that is extremely important to your business, so sending an email or hanging posters in the break room isn't enough.

Before rolling out, make sure that each of your company leaders have a good idea of how to integrate the core values into their specific area of the company. The leaders can then discuss this with the employees in their area of responsibility.

Schedule some time for the company to experience the core values training session. If you have a larger company, you may have to divide employees up by work area or by some other method.

Use the Core Values to Hire and Train Employees

Incorporating the core values into your hiring process is going to pay off big time for you. When you hire employees, who have P.h.D. and exemplify the core values, you will spend a lot less time dealing with employee drama and poor work performance. Make sure you review all of your job descriptions and rewrite them to reflect your core values.

You are probably going to have to create new company training material or at least significantly edit it. In fact, I know of a company that trains new employees on its core values even before the employees go through human resources training.

Incorporate Core Values into Performance Assessments and Reviews

In order to use your company's core values in the employee assessment process, you first have to identify the behaviors that are associated with each value. Keep in mind that the behavior for a core value may be very different from one area of the company to the next. For example, a core value that revolves around "teamwork" will look different in the warehouse/inventory area than it would in the human resources area.

Using *values-based performance management*, as it's often called, can be tricky. Watch out for being subjective. As you work to identify values-based behavior and actions, it can help if you talk to the higher performing employees in each role or area of the company to pin down realistic expectations.

Later in the book, I devote an entire chapter to performance management.

Core Values Should Be Front and Center

One way to emphasize your company's core values is in the employee handbook (also referred to as the "culture code"). You can also ask employees to write down their thoughts on one of the core values and how they follow it in their workplace (or even their personal life). This is excellent material for a newsletter or internal website, which are both effective ways to regularly reinforce your core values. Of course, don't forget the most obvious use of imagery and text displayed on the office walls or perhaps on wall-mounted monitors.

Companies with strong brands are also successful in working their core values into their sales, marketing, support, services, and other messaging. Just make sure that there are no discrepancies between the internal and external messaging.

Yet another way that you can highlight your core values is by celebrating and rewarding employees who are living one or more of the core values. This might be part of your performance management system or separate.

Regular Review Cycles

Immediately after the core values rollout, the team that worked on them should meet frequently to clarify issues and revisit the core values. As time goes by, it won't be necessary to meet as often, though it's still important to review your core values on a regular basis.

Difficulties and Pitfalls

I wish I could tell you that defining your core values is going to go smoothly, that nothing unpleasant will happen and the rollout will be wildly successful. That *might* happen, but it usually doesn't. Just so you're prepared, I've summarized a handful of common problems that might crop up.

Differentiate Yourself

You probably already know this, but certain words or phrases are frequently used as company core values. Think of words like "integrity," "service," and "community." There are a few problems with these words (and words like them):

❖ Using a single word, though succinct and simple, leaves a lot of room open for interpretation.

❖ The words have been overused to the point that they are meaningless.

❖ The words are commonly used, which means they don't have much impact.

To help with the first two problems, I recommend using short phrases, like "Integrity means we are open and transparent." To address the last bullet point, use a thesaurus to find different words with similar meanings. For example, when I look up "innovative" in a thesaurus, I see these equivalent words: advanced, pioneering, inventive, and original.

Don't Rush Through the Definition Process

Although the group may have approached the core values work as a "project" that can be checked off the To Do list when it's done, resist the urge to close it out too quickly. It's completely fine to let a few months go by while the group considers and reconsiders the core values that have been proposed. Everyone is going to have to live with these values for quite a while, so it's better to be right than to be "done."

Letting the Core Values Lapse

The core values are meaningless without people to breathe life into them. The core values have to be introduced and supported from the organization's leaders. Remember that leaders are always being watched, and people are quick to sense any hypocrisy.

Just as you will have a plan to introduce the core values to your employees and the world at large, you should have a plan for keeping these values alive on a day-to-day basis. If you don't know how to do this or you skimmed the last section ("Keep the Core Values in the Forefront") go back and read it.

Remember Core Values During Times of Transition

In times of trouble and crisis or as you scale, you need to figure out how to hold onto your core values. It's not a simple accomplishment when your company seems to be in a constant state of flux.

Some of the changes that can test a company's core values are:

❖ Leadership leaving or transitioning

❖ Employee layoffs

❖ Organizational merger and acquisition

❖ Rapid growth within the company

As part of the regular core value review process, have your leaders discuss how the core values will help with times of trouble or transition. That way, if the moment arrives, you'll be able to provide immediate support and reassurance to worried employees.

Choose High Performance Over Core Values

Another way that your core values can be tested is when you have employees who are high performers, but whose traits clash with those values. Make no mistake, if you notice it, then other employees and perhaps even your customers have noticed it.

One of your reasons for establishing core values is to set a standard for how you want your employees to behave. Unfortunately, probably sooner rather than later, there will come a time when an employee is found lacking in representing the core values.

This is when having core values can be painful and perhaps even seem detrimental to your business. But whether it's a genius programmer, smartest technician, or an account executive with the highest closing rate, you have to consider the long-term effects of having such a person represent your company. If such a person remains, you risk losing the respect and support of your employees and customers.

Chapter Summary

The influence of core values throughout your company cannot be underestimated. Core values can help guide your company in hiring new employees, choosing the next vendor, and even devising next year's strategic plan.

Furthermore, core values define your reason for being, your intentions, and what the company stands for. Customers who see your core values reflected in your employees' behaviors understand that they can rely on your business to do what it says it will do. People interested in your company's products and services can decide if your core values align with theirs.

After defining your core values, methodically infusing them into all aspects of your business is crucial. You created these values not only to describe your brand's character, but also as a guide for employees' (and management's) behavior. If the company as a whole can regularly refer to and live by its core values, they will find the values even more valuable when the company must scale, transition, or experience other changes.

You'll be glad you did the hard work of defining your company's core values; it makes the process of forming workplace culture that much easier. That's what I'll address in the next chapter.

In scaling your business, how did you get your team behind your vision?

MIKITA MIKADO

One of the things we did with my co-founder was to create a culture code that describes all of PandaDoc's values, our vision, mission, and the way we want to work and behave. Laying out clearly who we are and how we think helps to set the right expectations and inspires the right people right at the gate.

BOB MARSH

I'm a big believer in thought leadership as a sales and marketing strategy. For me that has meant a lot of writing, webinars, and public speaking. In doing so, I'm educating the market and our team in a way that aligns with our vision as I'm teaching people why what we do is important. When our team sees and hears me get that message out, it helps them understand why we do what we do. And the best way to prove the vision is reality and not fantasy is to get out in front of customers to hear how they are using our product successfully, and then share those stories back with others. That makes it more real.

Chapter 5 – Become Culturally Aware

You've probably heard the term *culture* bandied about so many times now that you wonder if there's not more of the *cult* in it than anything else. Even if you ignore or neglect the idea of "culture" at your workplace, it will still manage to establish itself organically as the result of employee interactions and events that occur at your company.

So, instead of allowing culture to grow at your company without your conscious effort or attention, it's better to understand what it is, as well as how you can create it and maintain it. You've already done the hard work of establishing your core values; defining the culture is very similar. (I'll explain later in this chapter the different between "core values" and "culture.")

If you're bothered by the artificiality of creating a culture, try to think of it as any other crucial element in your business, like the office equipment, underlying IT systems, business software, and so forth. These are all things that were chosen with deliberation and care, and it would be negligent to allow them to degrade over time. If you can think of culture in this way, as a real object instead of an amorphous concept, maybe you'll lose some of your reluctance to manufacture your own culture.

Speaking of amorphous concepts, in a bit I'm going to go over what culture actually is – and isn't. After that, you can find out the most typical terms used by organizations to describe their culture. I'll also give you some tips on creating your own culture and maintaining it as your company scales.

Why Culture is Important

Overall, a great company culture can affect everything... employee interactions, caliber of new hires, and satisfied customers. I mentioned earlier that no organization can afford to ignore or neglect its culture. Research and studies of companies with strong, positive work cultures show that they have lower job turnover rates, more productive employees, and higher operating income.

Lower Job Turnover Rates

Why lower job turnover rates? According to numerous studies, culture is closely related to employee engagement, which itself is nearly equivalent to "happy employees." Happy-plus-engaged employees are much less likely to quit their jobs. This has been proven to be true even if they are paid less than others in the same job positions at other companies (though only as long as the difference in pay isn't more than 10%). Less job turnover means less effort and time spent finding and training new employees.

Better Employee Chemistry

Another important product of a good, strong culture with happy employees is that there is better chemistry amongst themselves. Meaning less drama. Maybe even no drama (we can always hope).

On the flip side of employee engagement are those unhappy (disengaged) employees. Their lack of attention, low productivity, demoralizing attitude, and (sometime) outright sabotage can cost you thousands of dollars per year. If that doesn't keep you up at night, I don't know what will.

When your company has a constructive, dynamic culture, you are less likely to hire people who don't fit the culture. Firstly, your radar and intuition able to detect "false positives" and week out bad candidates. Secondly, unsuitable job applicants aren't likely to be attracted to a company with high standards for productivity and teamwork.

More Productive Employees

How about that "more productive employees" bit? Part of this result is due to the fact that working in an organization with a winning culture means that employees know what is expected of them in order to perform their job. They also know what that the company expects of them if in order to be promoted and receive salary raises.

Higher Operating Income

Then there's the higher operating income... several reasons for that. A firmly established culture with positive overtones provides a competitive advantage for a company because:

- ❖ It's difficult for a competitor to duplicate.

- ❖ It reinforces the company's brand and values, which makes it easier for consumers to remember it.

- ❖ The company is one where only the most sought-after employees want to work.

A higher operating income can also be due to the happier employees, who are more likely to have better relations with customers, thus producing more satisfied ones. Employees who are well pleased with their employers are apt to be more productive.

Attractive to a Large Pool of Job Candidates

Speaking of attracting talent, the next generation with clout due to sheer numbers is the *Millennials* – 75 million of them. They have gone on record in research and interviews stating that they prefer to work for a company with a strong work culture. So, there's yet another reason to have a definite work culture in place.

Organic Isn't Always Good

Finally, I'd like to add that in the absence of an established culture, one will grow organically – one that might not have all positive, wholesome descriptors. Some negative cultures that can develop revolve around cliques, complaining, cynicism, and complacency. And those are only the words that begin with the letter C!

What I Mean By Culture

An organization's culture is more than the half dozen perks it offers to employees, like lunchtime yoga, Pizza Fridays, and ping pong. It's also not the package of benefits represented by the glossy folder with your corporate logo that Human Resources slides across the desk at the employee's second interview. Nor can you say that culture is your company's open-office design in the modern loft aesthetic.

But, at the same time, these can all be part of your organization's culture.

Here's My Definition of Culture

So, really, what is culture? This is how I would describe it:

- ❖ Its about how management communicates.

- ❖ Its about how employees are treated when they succeed *and* when they fail.

- ❖ It's the ongoing interest in an employee's success or future at the company.

- ❖ It's what the company believes about its role in the marketplace.

- ❖ It's made up of the type of people the company typically hires.

- ❖ It's the company's stated values and vision of its future.

That last bullet point leads me to the next section...

The Difference Between Core Values and Culture

I hope you did some good work on defining your company's core values, because they are what shape the workplace culture. A society's culture is formed by its people. Since the same applies to a workplace culture, you'll find that the culture could change over time or have variations by department, locations, and so forth.

In contrast, a company's core values are not changeable; they are intrinsic to the company. If you changed a company's core values, it's almost like creating a new company.

If it helps, think of the workplace culture as the living, breathing embodiment of the company's core values. Or if that sounds too highbrow for you, you're allowed to discard it!

Does Your Company Have a Culture?

How do you know that culture exists at a company? Ask an employee two questions:

Question 1: Can you tell me what your culture is like?

Question 2: Is the culture written down anywhere, and how specific is it?

Regarding the first question, you might get an answer that's somewhat appropriate, like "Laid back" or "punishingly competitive" or "traditional and old school." You would know that there's a definite vibe at that company, something that can be described. At least there's something!

As for the second question, if you received a blank or bewildered look as an answer, you might have to ask the question of management or conclude that the organization does not have a definite culture.

In order for culture to exist at an organization:

❖ It has to be defined somewhere (so that its meaning doesn't get twisted or lost over time).

❖ Employees have to know about it and be able to describe it.

❖ It has to be consistently practiced.

Elements of a Strong, Vibrant Work Culture

As I strongly believe in the effectiveness and important of culture, I have collected some of the terms used to describe the culture of successful, well-known companies. I've assembled them below in alphabetical order. I hope you can use these as a springboard for shaping your own company culture.

What's interesting to realize is that most of these terms describe things that are free. The exceptions are providing fair salaries and paying for employee enrichment or development programs. That's amazing when you consider how important these concepts are to most employees.

For each of them, I've provided a brief explanation of how a company might interpret the concept, but if you decide to adopt a concept as your company's own, you'll want to put your own spin on it. Some of these are more open to interpretation than others.

So here you are... common elements adopted and owned by successful businesses:

Concept/Term	Definition/Suggestions
Accountability	Employees need to be accountable for substandard work or incomplete assignments. This also applies to teams, departments, and the organization as a whole.
Autonomy	This can refer to an employee's ability to work independently. A complementary term for autonomy is *collaboration*. The level required for both of these depends on the nature of the job being performed, of course, but an employee should be able to work well both alone and with others. Another way to think of this concept is in regard to how much power an employee has to make decisions without having to consult with upper management.
Collaboration	It's crucial for employees, teams, and departments to be able to work together without power struggles, drama, hoarding information, and one-upmanship. Another relevant topic around collaboration is the ability of teams and departments to work together to achieve a cohesive brand and message for the customer. Collaboration can become more complicated with a dispersed workforce, but it's not impossible.
Communication	This is such a broad term. It can relate to a company's commitment to regular meetings, its devotion to the best quality communication software, or an open-door policy. Related to communication is *transparency* (see below). You could also think in terms of always improving communication. We all think we're great communicators, but the fact is, we're probably just good talkers! The other half of the communication equation is learning how to listen and respond in ways that don't shut down communication. This applies to all methods of communication, such as texting, leaving voicemails, in-person and online chats, and so forth.

Fairness	This can be another difficult term to pin down. I think we tend to recognize fairness only in terms of "Hey! That's not fair!" In other words, we know it when we see it, though it's hard to describe succinctly. Fair pay for the same work is an obvious concept. Another way to practice fairness is to treat employees equally in handing out rewards or admonishment.
Familial / Friendly	The concepts of familial and friendly concern the work atmosphere. Although it would be difficult to replicate the sense of relief and relaxation one feels when entering their home, a work environment should feel supportive and pleasant as opposed to chaotic and stressful. Do you hire and retain people who strive to make others feel comfortable? Do employees and leaders have a true concern for others' personal lives? This becomes especially important when a person is dealing with problems at home or with their extended family.
Freedom	This is like autonomy but viewed from the other side of the table. Think of it as the opposite of micromanagement. A company that emphasizes freedom hires top-notch employees, gives them the appropriate tools, training, and resources, and then lets them do their job.
Fun	If there's anywhere that fun is desperately needed, it's our workplace. It can help balance out the occasional stress, unfortunate customers, and unexpected late nights. In order for a workplace to feel fun, you have to hire funny people, or at least people with a sense of humor. Although there are millions of ways to increase fun at your workplace, this is a concept that is highly subjective based on personality and background. For that reason, try to mix things up a bit so that everyone can enjoy the fun.

Goal setting	We've been taught since at least middle school the importance of setting goals, but it's easy to forget in the day-to-day business of just getting things done. Goal setting is definitely something that company leaders need to take ownership of, especially for goals related to getting more revenue, sales, and customers. It's also important to break down those super-large goals into more manageable achievements... all the way down to the employee level. A company that emphasizes goal-setting needs to work with employees to help them set goals that are challenging but not at the *Mission: Impossible* level. Employees who have clear, specific, and manageable goals are going to be more confident and focused in their work.
Integrity	Integrity is closely related to truthfulness. When you are a company or person with integrity, you always do what you said you would do. When you can be consistent in this way, you can earn the trust and respect of employees and customers.
Learning	Learning can comprise coaching, mentoring, seminars, and training. A company that commits itself to ongoing learning is telling its employees that they have a future with the company and opportunities for professional growth and enrichment.
Meaningful	Although this is a concept that is highly personal, it has to do with the idea that the work is making a difference in some way for the business, society, community, or the world. Even if the work is rather nondescript and mundane, it can be elevated to be meaningful if the business is itself doing work that is meaningful. I happen to believe that work is intrinsically meaningful if it enables us to support ourselves and our families; a bonus point if it is also challenging and engaging.

Passion	As with many of the other concepts in this list, passion is something that can be widely interpreted. Your business can be passionate about its main source of income, but it's important you support this concept in some concrete way so that it's not just a buzzword. Or you may decide that your company will only hire and retain people who are passionate about your company, the work itself, or their area of expertise (for example, electrical engineering or roasting coffee beans).
Praise & Recognition	Giving praise and recognition requires a personal touch. Some employees might be embarrassed by a public display of recognition, while other employees are highly motivated by sincere praise and recognition of their efforts. Also, keep in mind that there is surely a point where too much praise and recognition lessen its effectiveness.
Pride	Some care needs to be used with this term. What pride means to a company should be carefully explained, perhaps by associating it more closely with passion, learning, and the desire to always do better.
Results	I like this term best when it's used with "accountability." This term is closely related to accomplishment (a term that isn't in this list, but I had to stop somewhere!).
Transparency	A company that is transparent gives as much information to its employees and customers as it can. I mentioned this term up above in relation to "communication" because the two naturally go together; in most cases, when you're being transparent, it's because you are communicating information. Of course, you can also be transparent in your business operations, for example, by resolving not to use certain shady tactics common in your industry.

Trust	Trust is an enormously important concept, not just in the workplace, but woven into the fabric of our culture. Trust is easily shattered; for that reason and many others, a company that wants to use trust as its foundation has its work cut out for it.
	For a business to embody and exemplify trust, everyone has to trust the decisions and actions of others. Employees have to trust that leaders are doing the right thing, and leaders have to trust that employees will get the job done right.
Truthfulness	This one is closely aligned with "transparency." It's easy to be truthful when you are communicating positive or good information. But something to consider is how you'll handle truthfulness when the truth is unpleasant (for example, when providing constructive criticism during an employee review).

Create a Winning Culture

Ideally, it's best to start out with a defined, firm culture, but remain open to tweaking it as your business scales. This is effective even if you are starting out from scratch with just yourself as the one employee or if you have unfortunately let the culture lapse into a dog-eat-dog chaotic mess. If the latter is the case, the best approach is to tease out the most positive concepts from that mess while working to eliminate the destructive elements.

Whatever the situation, in order for employees and leaders to feel like they are a part of a culture, it's best if they have some say in establishing it.

Whatever culture you devise and maintain, it obviously has to be in tune with your own personal values. If not, I don't see how you could summon the enthusiasm and motivation needed to support it. So, you are going to have to do some self-evaluation as you wade through all the possible cultural concepts of your business. There's no need to go into psychotherapy but keep yourself attenuated to any of those concepts that cause you to flinch or leave you indifferent, even if you know them to be "good" ones.

Since the culture starts with you as the company leader, besides using the concepts I covered in the previous section, you can also look into your past for inspiration. How about places you've worked before... what did you like or dislike about the culture or atmosphere of those businesses? Look at others (mentors, parents, colleagues) whose work ethics you admire... can you pin down what it is that you like? If you have started a business before – whether it failed or went on successfully – what can you extract from there that worked or didn't work?

You can start by holding informal discussions, just to see what you're dealing with. Pin down the attitudes, behaviors, and actions that are and are not valued by your employees.

It might start out as confusion and dissent but try to narrow down what you think best articulates what your company is trying to accomplish. When you feel like you have a manageable set of concepts/terms, you can use more formal meetings or surveys to narrow down your choices.

When you believe you are really there, plan a celebration with your crew to reward the hard work and mark the new phase your company is entering. Whatever concepts or terms you have chosen to describe your culture should be written down to keep the message from being distorted.

Maintain a Winning Culture

Like anything of importance in life, your company's culture must be nurtured so that it can grow stronger. It's like a great marriage or a long-lasting friendship. It doesn't just happen... you have to work on it.

But the culture isn't really about work. You can use your culture to have fun at work. For example, it can give you reasons to praise others when you catch them exemplifying your company's culture. Or let's say a customer writes a testimonial, praising your team for demonstrating the concepts central to your culture. Do I really need to tell you this is a reason to celebrate?

You'll also need to give a newly established culture some time to evolve. After all, you'll probably hire more employees, or your company might change direction.

Encourage Regular Communication

One way to strengthen your company's culture is to communicate with each other regularly. Employees should have tools for communication beyond just email, such as instant messaging and video conferencing. Those jokes about the chit-chat around the water cooler have persisted for a reason, after all. Even small talk can help to strengthen culture.

One thing to think about is the communication between departments, who need to remain consistent in brand messaging for the customer. If communication silos have developed, your customer will receive mixed messages about your company.

Hire Employees Who Think Differently

One relatively simple way to perpetuate your company's culture is through the hiring of new employees. Although the temptation may be great, avoid hiring people who think like you or have a similar personality. Instead, look at your strengths and weaknesses, and hire people who can provide what is lacking. You don't need to sacrifice your personal or cultural values but look for perspectives that can support your company's culture while still providing a different point-of-view.

A workplace culture is often the result of how team members interact with each other. Keep this in mind when you hire new employees. Prospective hires may say they support your company's values, but the real clues can be found in their past motivations and behavior, which aren't difficult to discover if you take advantage of your social and business network.

If your workplace culture has shaped itself and retains negative features, understand how damaging this can be to the newly established culture. No matter how valuable an employee's past contributions and performance, it may be necessary to let them go if they don't fit with the culture.

Chapter Summary

Although many workplace cultures appear to have developed organically, it's much more likely that they are the result of considerable thought, analysis, and consensus. While it does make the concept of culture seem less romantic, it doesn't diminish the power of a positive business culture to:

- ❖ Lower job turnover rates

- ❖ Attract high-quality job candidates

- ❖ Keep employees engaged

- ❖ Satisfy customers

- ❖ Enhance your company's brand

It's risky business to allow your workplace to establish its own culture. As your company's leader, you must take the reins and lead your team to discover what aspects it will emphasize.

The difficulty isn't in finding the concepts that represent your company's values and vision, it's in narrowing them down and presenting them in such a way that it enhances your brand and resonates with your customers. This must be done without violating your own personal values or those of your employees. By inviting your employees to join in the discovery and definition of your workplace culture, they will be more likely to believe in it and embody it in their day-to-day activities.

It's true that the idea of "culture" loses some of its glamour when dissected here in this chapter, but the advantages of having a definite, clear culture are so obvious that I think it's worth it. Don't you?

Share one time when you took a chance and it paid off in your business.

MIKITA MIKADO

The biggest time I took a chance was when I moved to the United States at the age of 19, without any friends here and only $400 in my backpack. That definitely paid off.

BOB MARSH

In mid-2016 as I was meeting with more of our customers, I began to see that they were using our technology and they liked it, but it wasn't completely ingrained into the fabric of how they were running their teams. I saw this as a risk, and it was going to prevent us from accomplishing our mission of being a core part of how any sales team is managed – to be the management operating system for a sales organization.

An insight I heard from some of our better customers was that they were using our KPI management capability to run their team meetings and one-on-ones with salespeople. I'm a huge believer in hands-on coaching and that you must use data to help guide (not lead) your conversations, so saw an opportunity to build a coaching capability right into our system. This required us to redirect most all our engineering team to getting a coaching product into market as quickly as possible.

That was a risk, as there were many other capabilities a lot of our customers were asking about. Even our team members were seriously questioning why we were doing this because customers weren't directly asking us for a "coaching product." But through customer and product conversations, I firmly believed that was what our customers and the market needed, so we went forward, and it's made a huge difference. In fact, it has completely changed the way we go to market and message our entire offering. Some customers even said, "Now that you have this coaching piece, all the other parts of your product make more sense!"

Now in 2019, there is more talk than ever in the market about the importance of an effective coaching relationship between sellers and managers, and I see us being right in the middle of that.

Chapter 6 – Only Hire P.h.D.'s

What do I mean by P.h.D.?

If you don't know me, then you might think that "P.h.D." stands for the high-level degree of Doctorate of Philosophy. Actually, I'm referring to passion, hustle, and drive – the essential traits you need to consider before hiring anyone at your company.

Hiring for these traits is more important than hiring for certain job skills. In fact, I believe it is the difference between companies that are highly successful and companies that are just mediocre.

Listing very specific job requirements in order to find job candidates is like looking through a fixed telescope – you'll only see a small portion of the landscape. If you hire only based on specific skills, you might have smart employees, but not all of them will have the ability to work at the level you expect. Some of them might not be able to work well with others – definitely bad news.

When you hire for passion, hustle, and drive, you are more likely to have employees who support your workplace culture. If you'll remember in the previous chapter, one of the ways I describe workplace culture is that it's "made up of the type of people the company typically hires." Whatever your workplace culture may be, the traits of passion, hustle, and drive will only enhance it.

But before I jump into the topic of P.h.D.'s, I want you to ask yourself if it's the right time to hire an employee.

Do You Really Need an Employee?

If you find yourself in the pleasurable yet stressful position of having too much business to handle, you have my congratulations and my sympathies. You're obviously doing something right, so it might be time to consider hiring an employee to help.

However, hiring an employee isn't something to be done quickly or desperately. The cost of hiring a bad employee can literally cost you thousands of dollars. It could even damage your business's reputation or relationships with customers.

Although it may seem that the only way out of your frenzied 80-hour work week is to hire an employee, I encourage you to look at other options first. Hiring an employee involves a serious time and money commitment. It's worth it to look at alternatives before making the big hiring plunge.

Look for Efficiency Gaps

First, consider whether you are working as efficiently as you can. Look at the technology you're using. If you're using older software, familiarize yourself with the features of the latest version. Consider upgrading if there's a new feature that can help complete tasks faster. Or, if you aren't using technology at all, research what technology is out there that could help you.

If your business involves creative work like writing, art, or graphical design, make sure you're scheduling that type of work when you are freshest and at your best. Save the dull "grunt work" for those times when your creative energy wanes and you need a brain break.

Consider whether your workflow is as efficient as possible. If you're falling behind on certain tasks, such as social media marketing or paying the bills, put these tasks on your schedule at regular intervals. Make sure your work space is uncluttered and the tools you need are nearby.

Outsource Mundane Tasks

Is it possible to outsource any tasks that you dislike or aren't good at? Well, yes. You can find freelance accountants, bookkeepers, schedulers, and virtual assistants. Many of these freelancers work online (remotely) and at reasonable rates. Other online tasks that you can outsource include data entry, research, proofreading, software programming, and customer service.

It doesn't make sense for you to spend time doing something when you can pay someone less to do it. The time you save can be spent bringing in more revenue for your business.

Another reason it might be a good idea to outsource a project or task instead of hiring an employee is if you suspect the workload might not remain steady. This might be difficult to evaluate, but it's something to keep in mind. If you have any doubt that the work may slack off, you don't want to go through the trouble of hiring an employee, only to fire them a few months later.

Some Considerations Before Hiring

Let's assume you've carefully considered your business and situation, fixed as many efficiency gaps as you can, and don't believe a contractor or freelancer is the way to go. You want to hire someone, but before you move forward, there are a few more considerations.

Can You Afford an Employee?

If you really need the stability and consistency of a full-time employee, there are important considerations. The most important one is: Can you afford it?

Besides paying an employee's salary, there are taxes you must pay on their behalf (Social Security, Medicare, and unemployment) at the federal and state level. Depending on what type of job you are hiring for, you may have to purchase office equipment, a computer, and software. Also, if you live in an area where it's hard to find good workers, to make your job position more appealing you may have to pay for some benefits, such as healthcare and paid time off.

You also need to consider the time commitment involved in hiring, training, and managing an employee. You'll spend time filing taxes (monthly or quarterly), filling out paperwork, and keeping up-to-date on any other requirements that apply to taxes and labor laws.

To Hire or Not to Hire – Friends and Family

There's a "bright side and a dark side" to hiring family or friends.

On the bright side, you already know this person. You can skip the background check, and you don't need references. Maybe this person has a skill set that you don't have, which would really come in handy. There are even some tax benefits you can take advantage of if you hire a child or a spouse, though you'd need to check with a tax advisor first.

Furthermore, if you intended from the beginning to establish a family-owned business, it certainly makes sense that the employee would be someone from the family or a close friend. Hiring family into a small business is part of the process of carrying the business on to the next generation.

The dark side of hiring family or friends into your business is the same old story about mixing business with your personal life. Hiring a friend or loved one can be potentially dangerous to your personal relationship. It can make getting together at family or social events uncomfortable. By crossing the work-home line of separation, you might lose the ability to keep those two places separate.

If this is your first employee, hiring someone with whom you have a personal relationship might not be a problem because it's just the two of you. But later, you might hire on more employees who are not friends or family. These people might regard even your most innocent remarks and actions as nepotism.

If you have good reasons for hiring a family member or friend into your business, here are a few things to keep in mind:

❖ You should hire this person for a position that matches their skill set.

❖ From the beginning, make it clear (in writing) that advancement in the business is based on merit and not relationships.

❖ If possible, have the person start out as a paid intern or part-time. This gives both of you the chance to see if it can work without a major investment of time or money.

❖ The family member or friend should already have work experience in the "real world" and the appropriate education.

❖ A family member or friend in a managerial position must keep up-to-date on the latest business ideas and practices. This can easily be

67

accomplished if they belong to an industry or career-related organization.

Why Would Anyone Want to Work for You?

In the previous chapter, I mentioned that when people are looking for a new job position, the workplace culture is usually an important consideration for them. People do like to work for smaller companies and companies that are scaling up. They also enjoy the challenges of helping a business grow.

Another consideration for job seekers are perks. If you're small or just starting to scale up, you must realize what you're up against in terms of larger companies. Paid time off, free lunches, health club memberships, and on-site coffee shops are just some of the perks that larger companies now offer employees.

Forewarned is forearmed. Just as you will be asking job candidates what they can offer to your business, they will ask the same of you. So… what can you offer an employee who works for your business?

Granted, some of what you can offer are the intangibles, such as helping to shape the direction of the business, faster advancement and more responsibilities, and maybe even bragging rights for being one of the first employees. People want to feel like they are contributing to something that matters, so it's important for you to be able to "sell" the vision you have for your business. Furthermore, people like to feel their contributions are valued, and this is much easier at a smaller business.

If you can't compete with the larger companies in terms of salary, there are still several benefits you can offer to a new employee:

❖ Working from home

❖ Working flexible hours

❖ Stock options or equity in the business

❖ Very casual dress code

❖ Ability to choose their own technology

❖ Ongoing professional development (see Chapter 7)

Depending on your industry, you may be able to offer even more than that, such as free meals or deep discounts on your products and services.

Where to Look for Mr. or Ms. Right

If you aren't in a rush to hire, you can first look for an employee by putting out the word to your network. To encourage your network to help you out, offer a monetary bonus to the person who refers you to a person you hire.

Along the same lines, after you have hired some employees, you can ask them to refer potential employees to you. Make sure your employees know that you are looking for people who have the same traits of passion, hustle, and drive. It's a good idea to formalize your employee referral process by documenting and tracking it... even making a game or contest out of it.

Be careful to not "poach" an employee from someone you know well. Business is business, but there are plenty of job candidates out there, so why risk alienating an acquaintance?

If you are forced to post the job online or in a newspaper, make sure to use a "code word" that the job candidate must use in their email or cover letter. This helps weed out the people who blindly respond to any job posting without regard to their abilities.

Hire for Passion, Hustle, and Drive (P.h.D.)

Now that I've covered the practical considerations involved in hiring employees, I can get back to my main topic, which is hiring people who demonstrate passion, hustle, and drive.

Quick Definitions

Before I describe these traits in more detail, I want to give a brief overview of what I mean by passion, hustle, and drive, just so we're on the same page. I covered this in the Introduction, so if you think it seems familiar – you're right!

❖ Passion—An enthusiastic interest or love you have for something, which can be specific (a passion for graphic design) or general (a passion for learning).

❖ Hustle—Denotes urgency and the ability to not only work hard but work smart.

❖ Drive—The energy or ability to keep going through obstacles or failures.

In the following sections, I describe in more detail what I mean by passion, hustle, and drive. After that, make sure you read the section on how to find job candidates with these vital traits.

Passion

As I mentioned earlier, passion can be specific or general. You can look for people who have a specific passion related to their job tasks (such as a passion for balancing the books) or have a general passion for something related to your company (such as a passion for your company's product).

People who have a passion for something related to your company can only benefit it because:

❖ They have an interest in the subject that helps them sustain hustle and drive. Hustle and drive require quite a bit of physical and emotional energy, and passion is the foundation that supports them.

❖ Their interest in the subject means they view any problems that pop up not as a burden, but as interesting puzzles to solve. This desire to resolve issues also means that they will be scanning the virtual landscape for ways to prevent those problems in the first place.

❖ They are often interested in the subject to a degree that they are constantly looking to learn more about it or frequently thinking about it. This adds value to your company because the candidate has the potential to be a topic expert or even a thought leader. They might also be on the lookout for different ways to use your product or service or new ways to get more customers.

Hustle

While passion is cerebral, hustle is more about action. As I mentioned earlier, hustle suggests working with urgency, working both hard and smart. Someone who shows the trait of hustle knows where to best spend their time to achieve results.

Hustle is not about putting your nose to the grindstone and working, working, working. Although hustle is more about action, it does involve the most important part about it is that it involves thinking about how to do the job in the most efficient or effective way (i.e., work smart).

Someone who shows the trait of hustle is concerned with the results of their job tasks. They are likely to get a lot of pleasure from setting goals related to their work, although I don't necessarily think this means that they have to be competitive with others. Someone who is competitive in beating their previous results or shows continuous improvement can make an excellent employee.

Drive

While passion is about an enthusiastic love of something and hustle is about getting things done, having driven is a specific type of energy or ability to keep going through obstacles or failures. This type of mental and emotional stamina can be part of someone's overall personality – highly desirable to have in an employee – or it can be more narrowly focused on achieving certain goals.

In your case, you definitely want someone who at least shows the drive to succeed at work, both in terms of their career and their day-to-day tasks. An employee with drive must be able to:

❖ Get up and keep going, even after making mistakes or experiencing failure.

❖ Work through the tedious parts of their job without giving in to boredom or apathy.

❖ Understand how their participation at work contributes to the overall goals and vision of the company.

How to Find P.h.D. Job Candidates

Although hiring people who have the traits of passion, hustle, and drive is very important, keep in mind that other factors are also important, such as finding people who are a good cultural fit for your company. There is plenty of good advice out there about hiring qualified and conscientious employees, so in this section I will give you tips specifically for detecting the traits of passion, hustle, and drive.

Look for Passionate People

Conventional interview questions make it difficult to detect passion. A prepared job candidate will have memorized the responses to these types of questions. There's nothing wrong with someone who has prepared for a job interview in this way. It certainly shows that they can prepare ahead of time and have a desire to do well at the interview. It's just that scripted answers are a poor indicator of passion.

I have noticed that people who are passionate about a subject are unendingly curious about it. Therefore, you can look for curiosity and a love of learning when interviewing job candidates. Try to steer the interview into areas where the job candidate can discuss their passion. You'll be able to gauge how deep that person's interest is in the subject and perhaps their methodology for learning or educating themselves.

A warning… often job candidates appear to be passionate but are actually just excited to be involved in the interview process or at the prospect of getting a new job. Make sure you distinguish between passion and plain ol' excitement.

Discover People Who Can Hustle

You may find that some people show hustle in everything they do – from morning until night. You'll realize you're in the presence of this type of person just by having a general conversation with them. Such people are rare, so it's more realistic to look for someone who can hustle when it comes to their job tasks.

You can find people who hustle by looking at their previous employment. Those who have worked in service-related industries – especially as waiters and waitresses – know how to quickly prioritize tasks as well as re-prioritize when the circumstances change.

Another way to discover candidates who hustle is to look for those who know how to analyze information, have experience in troubleshooting, and otherwise know how to "sort the wheat from the chaff."

As I mentioned in the "Hustle" section earlier, people who can hustle are typically very gratified by seeing results in their work. You can look for people who have set goals for themselves, both in their private lives and in their careers. Someone interested in continuous improvement (in job processes, in their personal life, etc.) will likely be able to hustle.

Find People with Drive

You can often find people who are driven by noticing an associated trait, perseverance. This is someone who can keep going, even after falling flat on their face. Of course, everyone is disappointed after failing to meet a goal or making a mistake – we're only human – but what you need to discover are the people who can quickly recover, learn from what went wrong, and keep moving forward.

Besides associating perseverance with drive, you can also search for those who demonstrate a certain humbleness in being able to take on what might be considered menial tasks. I don't mean that you should look for someone who's willing to be a grunt! What I mean is, there's a certain amount of tedium with every job, so you want to be sure a person can work through the drudgery in order to meet a goal or fulfill their job responsibilities.

How to Interview Job Candidates for P.h.D.

The Hiring Matrix later in this section guides the interviewer in ensuring the interviewee has characteristics of passion, hustle, and drive so the right people are hired in the company.

The interviewer should pick at least three questions from each of the categories below in addition to creating skill-based questions (which varies depending on the role they are hiring for).

How to Interview for Passion

- ❖ Cheerful personality

- ❖ Answer questions with zest

- ❖ Ample research about the company and the industry

- ❖ Ask about their future goals (passionate people always have foresight and want to achieve more)

- ❖ Ask about knowledge or skills acquired recently (passionate people always want to enrich their inner soul)

- ❖ Ask about hobbies and interests (passionate people are not only eager at work, but also keen to engage in meaningful hobbies)

❖ Look for examples for all the skills that the candidate says that he/she possesses

❖ Non-verbal cues are just as important (firm handshake, confident posture, nodding when listening)

How to Interview for Hustle

❖ Give me an example of a time where a decision you made turned out to be a horrible idea. What happened, or what did you do about it? (Someone that is determined to succeed has the needed hustle.)

❖ When is the last time something didn't go as planned? How did you react?

❖ Then we want to look for personal stories, as every hustler has an origin story. You want to ask questions like: Tell me about a personal project that you are truly proud of.

❖ What is one of the most inventive things you did as a child that you still talk about today?

❖ Hustlers know how to climb the ladder of success. There is a constant thirst – a hunger for growth. Ask questions like: Have you ever been promoted? Why or why not?

❖ Have you gotten a job for which you were not qualified? (Hustlers will often throw themselves into the deep end and figure out how to swim.)

❖ Lastly, you want to measure for getting the job done. Questions to ask are: Have you ever asked for an extension on an assignment or task? Why or why not?

❖ When was the last time, if ever, that you stayed late at the office or at school? What was it for?

❖ Hustlers back their suggestions with evidence, research, or experiments. When looking at our company/product, what is something that you think should change? Why? (Hustlers are not afraid to speak their mind and will let you know what they are thinking.)

How to Interview for Drive

❖ We want to see if they set goals for themselves and how they work to achieve them, so a good question could be: How do you measure your goals?

❖ When was the last time you got into a competition?

❖ Think back to the time that you lost a sale? What did you do to recover?

❖ Tell me about a job that you enjoyed the least. What part of it did you enjoy the least?

❖ What work environment do you work best in? Tell me about a time when you worked in this environment.

All-In-One Question

Over-encompassing question that will show elements of passion, hustle, and drive together: What drives you crazy? Based on the answer, you can see how the candidate thinks about their motivations, people/things that make them happy or bug them, and if they respond positively or negatively to different types of work scenarios.

Hiring Matrix to Use As a Guide

How To Hire People With P.h.D.

Passion ·······························

The interviewee has...

- [ ] Cheerful personality

- [ ] Answer questions with zest

- [ ] Ample research about the company and the industry

- [ ] Ask about their future goals (passionate people always have foresight and want to achieve more)

- [ ] Ask about knowledge or skills acquired recently. (Passionate people always want to enrich their inner soul)

- [ ] Ask about hobbies and interests (passionate people are not only eager at work, but also keen to engage in meaningful hobbies)

- [ ] Look for examples for all the skills that the candidate says that he/she possesses

- [ ] Non-verbal cues are just as important (firm handshake, confident posture, nodding when listening)

🚀 Hustle ·······················

The interviewee can...

☐ Give me an example of a time where a decision you made turned out to be a horrible idea. What happened, or what did you do about it. (someone that is determined to succeed has the needed hustle)

☐ When is the last time something didn't go as planned? How did you react?

☐ Then we want to look for personal stories as every hustler has an origin story. You want to ask questions like: Tell me about a personal project that you are truly proud of.

☐ What is one of the most inventive things you did as a child (or talk) that you still talk about today?

☐ Hustlers know how to climb the ladder of success. There is a constant thirst – a hunger for growth. Ask questions like: have you ever been promoted? Why or why not?

☐ Have you gotten a job for which you were not qualified? Hustlers will often throw themselves into the deep end and figure out how to swim.

☐ Lastly you want to measure for getting the job done. Questions to ask are: Have you ever asked for an extension on an assignment or task? Why or why not?

☐ When was the last time, if ever, that you stayed late at the office or at school? What was it for?

☐ Hustlers back their suggestions with evidence, research or experiments. When looking at our company/product, what is something that you think should change? Why? - Hustlers are not afraid to speak their mind and will let you know what they are thinking.

⟨⟨⟩ Drive ·······················

The interviewee is...

☐ We want to see if they set goals for themselves and how they work to achieve them, so a good question could be:
How do you measure your goals?

☐ When was the last time you got into a competition?

☐ Think back to the time that you lost a sale? What did you do to recover?

☐ Tell me about a job that you enjoyed the least. What part of it did you enjoy the least?

☐ What work environment do you work best in? Tell me about a time when you worked in this environment.

☐ When was the last time, if ever, that you stayed late at the office or at school? What was it for?

☐ Hustlers back their suggestions with evidence, research or experiments. When looking at our company/product, what is something that you think should change? Why? - Hustlers are not afraid to speak their mind and will let you know what they are thinking.

Some Final Tips

During the interview process, it's better to talk salary in the beginning so that you're both on the same page. At that point, you can explain the other benefits that help make working for you more attractive.

Although salary is obviously important, if the person you really like and want is out of your salary range (but not too far), I think it's better to spend a bit more to get a good fit. If you try to save by going with your second or third choice, you could end up losing money instead through lack of productivity and bad morale.

If you're ready to make a job offer, take the time to ask around (discretely) about the job candidate. There's a chance someone in your network knows them and can either encourage or discourage your choice. If possible, check the person's references and, if relevant, their work samples.

After the hire, your job doesn't stop there! You'll need to keep good employee records. You'll also need to bring them on board in the right way. This is especially important if your business relies heavily on technology or processes.

One way to help reinforce the training is to have the new employee document your business procedures as they learn. (That is, if you haven't already documented them as I recommended in Chapter 1, "Is It Time to Scale?") When it's time to hire and train your next employee, you'll thank me!

Chapter Summary

Let's recap this chapter…

Before jumping on the hiring train, carefully consider if there are job tasks you can outsource to freelancers. You should also evaluate your processes to see if they are as efficient as possible.

Hiring an employee is an important financial commitment and hiring at the wrong time or hiring the wrong person can prove to be a serious blow to your company's finances. Make sure you can afford not only an employee's salary, but the benefits and perks associated with the job.

The job market is a competitive place for both employers and job seekers. With that in mind, you should write down the reasons why someone should want to work for your company. You can be sure that job candidates will ask for this information during the interview!

I strongly recommend you look for the traits of passion, hustle, and drive in anyone you are considering as an employee. Not only will this yield a high-energy and determined workforce, it will help shape a positive workplace culture as it is growing.

Your search for great candidates will be more fruitful if you use your social and business network to root out high-quality candidates. You can also ask employees for help in finding people who exhibit passion, hustle, and drive. These two methods often yield better results than posting the job online.

Tracking down job candidates and "testing" them for passion, hustle, and drive might seem more like an art than a science. It might seem simpler to hire people based on their skill set. However, if you use my recommendations from this chapter, you can gradually develop a job candidate search and vetting process that yields results.

What is the makeup of a successful sales manager?

SCOTT LEESE

Same as a successful salesperson, but less selfish. More joy from seeing others succeed than personal success. Patience to teach and mentor and a superior attention to detail.

RICHARD HARRIS

An unselfish and innate desire to help others improve and achieve their reps' goals before their own. This means being able to navigate the murky waters between leadership and friendship. Reps should not be your drinking and social friends every weekend, but you also cannot be a general sitting behind a desk and avoiding them either.

The best sales managers will always have their reps' backs when the time comes, even if they don't want to do that.

SAMAR BIRWADKER

Someone who complements their team. Most salespeople are quick-moving hustlers, making things happen. The sales manager should respect that hustle, likely having been there before, but also provide guardrails for their team to reach success.

KYLE PORTER

Relentlessly driven to serve others.

Chapter 7 – Invest in Your People

In the not-too-distant past, the unofficial policy of many companies in the United States was that professional development was the employee's concern. Furthermore, management generally believed that if they offered training and professional development to employees, the employees would eventually be tempted to seek greener pastures.

Thankfully, these perceptions are now understood to be outdated and – in the case of the previous sentence – absolutely untrue. Employees who receive training and are offered the opportunity to learn through enrichment or development programs are actually more loyal to their employers.

Employee loyalty is just one of the many benefits a business can reap when it classifies employee training and development an *investment* and not an expense. Because employees are your most important asset, you should invest as heavily as possible in their training and professional development.

The Benefits of Investing in Employees

In this section, I want to discuss how providing training, professional development, and other enrichment programs to employees will directly benefit your business. Although I realize you might already know about some of these benefits, the topic is so important that I want to reinforce it here. I also hope that by seeing these benefits in black and white, you'll be motivated to take definite steps in setting up your own development, enrichment, or training programs.

Hire and Retain the Best Employees

Programs that are designed to increase employees' knowledge and skills are considered a workplace benefit. People who enjoy learning and improving themselves will be more interested in working for your company. You'll get your pick of the brightest and most determined workers.

Accordingly, people who are not interested in learning and improving themselves (i.e., only interested in clocking in and clocking out of a nine-to-five job) will *not* be attracted to your organization. You'll be screening out these people with no effort on your part. Furthermore, you'll have a competitive advantage over those of your competitors that don't have enticing employee enrichment programs.

That's a triple win! Just look:

#1 Hiring and keeping better, brighter employees

#2 Screening out unmotivated job candidates

#3 Competitive advantage

Develop Company Leaders In-House

By working in-house with your employees to train them and improve their skill set, you are effectively grooming them for positions with more responsibility. These programs also give you the opportunity to observe employees, to discover their strengths and weaknesses and identify areas that need work. This is so much better than having to learn about weak areas through employee-customer interactions.

Also, by training employees and promoting them from within, you can lower your cost of employee acquisition. Better that the money you save is spent on employee bonuses, management training, or some other aspect to improve employee satisfaction.

Improve Employee Engagement and Loyalty

Employees who are bored with their jobs have sloppy work habits and bad attitudes. With their bad morale, they can upset the work of an otherwise healthy, productive team. If they have contact with customers, even worse.

You can prevent bored employees by offering professional development programs and constant access to training and learning. Even the best employees find some aspects of their job tedious, and these programs can give them something to look forward to as well as a sense of achievement.

Employees who are encouraged to better themselves at work feel appreciated, valued, and special. They will likely stay longer with your company and recommend friends and colleagues for jobs at your company. Additionally, engaged and loyal employees are more motivated and need less supervision.

Save and Earn Money

Recent studies support the idea that employee learning and development programs should not be considered an expense but an investment. One pair of business experts led a study that found the top quartile of organizations that invest in their employees have 40% more productive power. Besides improving productivity, employees who improve their skills help their employers by increasing sales and retaining customers.

As mentioned earlier, by promoting from within and retaining employees longer, you won't have to spend as frequently to acquire new employees. When an employee leaves, it can cost six to nine months of their salary to find a replacement. If your company is in an industry that typically has high employee turnover, that can cause some real damage in terms of revenue, profitability, and market position.

Encourages Future Planning

When you have to decide on what training or development programs to offer, you naturally think about the skills you need, not just now but in the future. For example, what kind of leadership skills will you need? What will customers need from employees? How will industry changes affect your current skill sets?

If you have already been providing professional development and/or training, what has worked in the past might not work in the near future because of industry or culture changes. You might need to attract a different type of employee, and your programs must reflect that if you are to attract them.

The value you receive from considering and making these important decisions have a ripple effect across your company. Not only are you more aware of what's coming, so are your team leaders and employees. By sharing this information with them, they will feel more interested in the company's future and motivated for those challenges that are just around the corner.

Increases Company and Employee Adaptability

Related to the previous section is the fact that employees who receive appropriate training for now and the future are going to be more adaptable. Whether individually, as a team, or part of a department, they can respond better to market changes and shifting customer needs. This can only help your organization become more successful in the long term.

Enhances Your Brand and Reputation

The fact that you provide programs to help your employees can go a long way in boosting your reputation with the general public, your customers, and the employees you already have. You won't even have to brag about it… this type of information has a way of organically traveling through the grapevine via conversations and social media.

Training and Other Development Programs

At minimum, you must have a formal training program. If you don't have one in place, new employees are not trained properly, and existing employees won't be able to consistently perform their job duties.

It's easier to create training material if you have already standardized your procedures for running your business and documented them. This may seem inhibitive to you or to your employees, but after it's done, they don't have to worry about the little details (that are often so important) of their day-to-day tasks. They are freed up to do more creative or business development tasks, and if there's a question about how a task or procedure should be done, the documentation provides the answer.

Who Creates and Delivers Training Material?

In general, it's better to not use the time of senior employees for training, as their time is better spent on doing their core job duties. For the most part, hiring a third-party company to create and deliver training isn't effective since they don't know your business, products, services, or processes.

Ideally, it's best to have an employee dedicated to providing training to new employees, but that's not always possible. One idea is to hire a consultant to help you create the training material. Then, for hands-on training, divide the training up amongst mid-level employees – using senior employees' time only when necessary and sparingly.

Training and Enrichment for Everyone

Enrichment, development, and training programs should be offered to all employees, hourly and salaried. Every aspect of work can be improved by training or professional development in such a way that it provides individual and company advantages.

It will be easier to deliver training material and other learning programs to employees if you take advantage of webcasts, podcasts, and just-in-time learning. Delivering information online makes it much easier to people to learn in the office, when traveling for work, or when working remotely.

Keep in mind that people learn in different ways and have various learning styles. Some prefer to read information, others like to listen to it, and yet others might want to watch a short video clip. Learning management systems (LMS) can help you create, manage, and even deliver training content. You can find LMS at all price points; the ones with more advanced features enable you to create quizzes and tests as well as monitor employee performance.

Link Learning to Your Company's Vision and Strategy

When creating your company's training material, it's important to emphasize how learning and training help to fulfill the company's strategy. People learn better if they understand the "why" behind what they're learning. Employees should be introduced to your company's strategic vision and goals as soon as possible, so why not during onboarding or training?

In order to accomplish your company's vision and goals, you also must determine what skills you can cultivate in-house and which ones you must outsource to freelancers or hire outright. This is yet another aspect of thinking strategically about your company, which I first wrote about back in Chapter 1. While planning for what you need today, you must also look to the future and what skills your organization will eventually need.

Provide Engaging Material

It should go without saying, but training and other development material should be interactive and interesting. Otherwise, what's the point? Employees will just tune it out and you'll be wasting your money. After new employees are trained, get their honest opinion on the training material (perhaps through anonymous surveys) and use that to tweak it.

Recognize Employees' Accomplishments

Another important aspect of training and development programs is to recognize each employee's progress. Most learning management systems have this feature, but even if they do, it doesn't hurt to do a bit extra to make employees glad that they put in the extra effort.

A Different Way to Invest in Your Employees

Up to this point, I have addressed the concept of investing in your employees as a matter of training or by teaching new ideas and skills. However, I wanted to mention two non-traditional ways you can invest in your employees – by giving them the gift of time and space for creative energy to flow.

Uninterrupted Time to Explore New Ideas

Another way in which you can invest in your employees is to give them the gift of more uninterrupted time. Knowledge workers are especially burdened with emails and meetings that disrupt their time such that there isn't any time left over for clear, deep thinking. Although it was once a modern fad to brag about one's ability to multitask, it's now understood that our brains cannot multitask (think of two things at the same time). We all need free time to plan, envision, or strategize.

If employees don't have this time, they tend to feel frustrated and might even burn out on their work. Obviously, by taking care of your employees in this way, you will benefit them and the organization.

If you'll remember, in Chapter 1, I stated how important it was for you to set aside blocks of time in order to think strategically about your business. To further emphasize this, in the same chapter ("Important Aspects of Scalability and Growth" section), I wrote:

> "[I]t's important to provide the means for you and your employees to encourage and exchange ideas. The workday environment should be conductive to sharing ideas...."

One of the resources I checked recently stated that during the day, knowledge workers only experience deep thinking time in increments of 20 minutes. If that's what we as a society are using as a basis for developing improvements in technology, operations, and other business systems, that's scary! Although it's true that great ideas often come in a flash (typically in the shower), we also need uninterrupted time to consider and develop them.

In all ways, strive to remove any internal complexity in your business that leads to unproductive interactions. Look for ways to streamline or quicken your business processes. For example, some companies are experimenting with Kaizen "events" to improve productivity. Other companies have replaced multiple meetings throughout the day with morning scrums or have shortened the product development lifecycle using Agile sprints.

You may not be able to do it every day, but it's crucial for your employees' sanity and your company's future to plan for innovation. After all, we can't always rely on the consistency of those shower ideas!

The Culture of Creative Energy

Along the same lines, to enable employees to improve themselves when they are working for you, you must initiate or sustain a culture that supports them as they explore new ideas or inspiration. It's not just about having a block of time; you must also consider the prevalent attitude (i.e., culture) in your organization. Does it encourage and appreciate thinking outside the box? What aspects of your workplace culture support it?

Employees will feel more inspired and energized when these building blocks of creativity are in place. Another way to encourage employee ingenuity is to provide good role models for it, such as through inspirational leadership.

One of the more striking facts that I recently came across stated that employees who are inspired are *twice* as productive as a satisfied employee and *more than three times* as productive as a dissatisfied employee. The way I see it, you can't afford to not provide the tools of inspiration to your employees!

Chapter Summary

I hope this chapter has impressed on you the significant value your organization will realize when it offers training and other formal professional development programs to its employees. You'll get the best employees, groom potential leaders in-house, save on employee acquisition costs, enhance your brand and reputation, and be better prepared for future challenges.

Besides training new employees on their day-to-day tasks, make sure you incorporate into training material your company's vision and goals. It's easier to remember *how* to do something if you understand *why* you're doing it!

You should offer training to all of your employees, no matter if they are salaried or hourly. However, you shouldn't use all of your employees to provide training. Learning management systems can help deliver training and make it available to a wider audience, such as those who work remotely or on second or third shifts. You can also take advantage of such technology to track employee progress; make sure you let employees know you appreciate their efforts to better themselves through learning.

Providing enrichment opportunities to employees isn't restricted to just training. Another way to help employees tap into their potential is to give them larger blocks of "creative time," access to inspiring leaders (especially through mentoring), and a stimulating atmosphere that encourages them to think up new ideas without restriction or criticism.

What should the main focus of senior sales leadership be?

SCOTT LEESE

Set the course for the team. Surround yourself with excellent people and constantly work to remove obstacles out of their way. Fight for them and get to know them so you can better understand their motivations.

RICHARD HARRIS

Three things... first, provide quality data to the reps – don't make the reps find the data.

The other two points are making sure training and coaching is built into the sales culture every single week. There is nothing more important than that. If you have good data and good training and coaching, the rest will take care of itself. It's a lot like parenting. The more quality time I spend with my kids, the better they will become in life. It doesn't mean I am going to solve all their problems for them, but I will teach them how to be good problem solvers.

SAMAR BIRWADKER

There is always a bigger picture than quarterly goals. Yes, those goals are necessary to get to the end-of-year success but being short-sighted and thinking in three-month intervals can cause sales teams to lose the forest for the trees. It's the senior sales leadership team who should be providing a North Star for their teams for the long-term goals of the organization and how to reach them.

KYLE PORTER

Hiring the people who will enable you to make the biggest impact on the customer.

Chapter 8 – Set Expectations with Performance Management

A performance management system consists of the processes for working with each employee to plan, monitor, and review their work objectives and goals.

You may have been exposed to performance management systems in the past, with various results in effectiveness. Maybe you were an employee who received an employee performance review each year. Or maybe you were in upper level management and had the responsibility for appraising employees who worked under you.

Although you have to give a nod to your previous places of employment for trying to evaluate employees on a regular basis, I personally don't think one annual performance review contributes much to an organization's success.

A successful performance management system consists of so much more than an annual performance review. I'm going to cover the components of this type of system as well as discuss the reasons and benefits of having one at your organization.

It can be tricky to organize and maintain an effective performance management system such that it aligns with your overall short-term and long-term goals. However, it's really the most effective way to generate consist productivity and efficiency improvements.

Reasons and Benefits

Overall, the reasons for and benefits of having a well-run and accepted performance management system are very similar to that of investing in your employees (covered in the previous chapter). You can retain better employees, recognize a competitive advantage, identify future company leaders in-house, and improve employee engagement and loyalty.

That might be enough to convince you, but if you're still not persuaded that a performance management system will add value to your business, keep reading. I've got some convincing reasons!

Identifies Your Organization's Competencies and Skill Gaps

Part of creating an effective performance management system is to nail down exactly *what* performance is expected and *how* it is to be achieved. If your employees have the skills necessary to perform their jobs at the highest level, that's great! If not, you must define what skill gaps exist.

It could be that you'll have to implement or access additional training or professional development programs, but at least you know what you don't know and are in a better position to fix it. This is much more desirable than being blindsided in the middle of a project when you realize your team members don't have the skill set to successfully complete it. Or how about completing the project and discovering that it was done incompetently?

The forward-looking attitude of a performance management system means you can identify employees who need more training or mentoring and be better prepared for what's around the corner.

Provides Visibility on Performance Expectations

Providing visibility on performance expectations means that employees know what their job responsibilities are. This includes doing their job tasks to a certain level of quality, which can be measured in various ways (referred to as metrics).

It seems obvious, but I'll state it here: you can't expect an employee to do their job well if they don't know exactly what that job is! Employees who know what is expected of them can better assess (and self-correct) their own work, which leads to better productivity and performance.

Another reason that it's important to nail down this information is to have a baseline for evaluating an employee's performance. After measuring performance against expectations, you'll be able to provide feedback that is more precise, specific, and therefore more helpful.

Recognizes and Rewards Employees for Excellent Job Performance

When you are able to recognize excellent performance, you can reward the employee, who will be motivated to continue in the same vein. This is also a signal for other employees who aren't performing as well; it encourages them to work harder.

Employees who understand their worth to a business and have their value acknowledged are more likely to be loyal to your company, thus staying on longer. The side benefit of this is that you can save on employee acquisition costs. In addition, when it's time to promote someone into a position with more responsibility, you can better match the right employee to the position because you already know you can depend on their job performance.

Links Your Business Vision and Goals to Day-to-Day Activities

Although the above reasons and benefits are important, the most important reason to put a performance management system in place is to ensure that there is a strong link between your business objectives and your employees' day-to-day activities.

One of the primary motivators for employees is the desire to do well at their job and feel like they are making a valuable contribution. A successful performance management system helps them understand how their day-to-day actions affect the company's bottom line.

We'll discuss your company's vision, goals, and priorities later in this book, but the benefits of having all employees pulling in the same direction are obvious. Such a company can become a strong competitor in the marketplace. It will also recognize improved productivity, savings, and performance.

At a higher level, with a proper performance management system, management has an early warning system in case there's a problem with how it's pursuing its objectives. Instead of waiting for the end of the fiscal year, they can instead make corrections to keep the business on track.

Documents and Supports Personnel Decisions

A good portion of a performance management system involves defining job performance expectations. At minimum, the notes and documentation generated from this system keeps everyone on the same page – employees, managers, human resources, etc. If someone remembers a certain event taking place differently, it's a simple matter to check the performance management system documentation. In this way, it can help resolve disputes and create less conflict for supervisors and management.

A performance management system can also help you make the decision whether to retain or terminate an employee since you'll have the details of the employee's performance right in front of you. In the case of poorly performing employees, it's better to let them go sooner rather than later, and the performance management system makes it easier to spot them. Along those same lines, the documentation from a performance management system can be used to head off a job-related lawsuit.

On a more positive note, the performance management system also helps document career paths, which help to motivate employees. It's also useful for making promotion and salary decisions.

Components of a Performance Management and Accountability System

There's a lot more to this type of system than you would expect. I've included what I think are the essential components here.

Prepare Management

Managing employees and their work is a complex task that requires observation, objectivity, and discernment. Equally important is the ability to:

❖ Detect problems that affect performance

❖ Develop others through motivation and coaching

❖ Deal with conflict

Employees have a wide variety of traits, intelligence, abilities, and experiences. Managers must tailor their input, support, and supervision in such a way to get the best result from each employee. If your managers have not been in their position very long or if they have never worked with performance management systems, I strongly suggest that you provide some training for this important role.

Set Goals

Setting goals is a collaborative effort between the manager and the employee, though of course not all objectives are open to discussion. Goals give employees a reason to come to work every day. They also want to feel as if they are making valuable contributions to the organization and are performing well.

It's not just enough to tell employees, "Your time and effort is a contribution to the overall organization." That's vague, unhelpful, and they've probably heard it a hundred times. Instead, employees need to specifically understand how their individual goals fit into the larger organization. Obviously, in order to do that, the goals need to be written clearly and objectively, and they really must contribute to the success of the business strategy.

Ensure That Employee Goals Are Aligned with Your Strategy

Although we haven't yet covered the topic of your company's strategic goals and operational plan, here's a simplified explanation of how to link them to individual employee goals:

1. Upper management establishes the general business strategy.

2. Upper management also creates the organization-wide goals that support the general business strategy.

3. Based on the organization-wide goals, the departmental managers set goals for their departments.

4. Each manager shares the overall goals with their department and meets with employees to identify individual performance goals and plans.

It's important that departmental managers have access to all of the other manager's goals. This ensures there is no overlap and reduces conflict. The members of different departments can see where they support each other, and no one is working at cross purposes.

Goal Setting 101

When defining individual goals, you can use the person's job responsibilities (based on the job description) as a reference and guide. A goal has two important elements: *what* and *how*. The *what* specifies any deadlines, the expected quantity and/or quality, and any other specifications. The *how* refers to the actions used to achieve the outcome.

Using established goals as a basis, performance planning sets the stage for the year by communicating objectives and setting an actionable plan to guide the employee to successfully achieve goals.

You can define both long-term and short-term goals; just make sure that a goal is always paired with an action plan for how the goal will be reached. You can also assign priorities to goals by giving the important ones more weight.

Another factor in setting a goal is to identify any obstacles that might prevent the goal from being met. Obstacles can range from a lack of knowledge or skills to lack of equipment or supplies. Whatever the case, you must also describe a plan for overcoming them.

Determine Employee Performance Measurements

There are many different ways to measure employee performance and not enough room in this chapter to cover all of them. However, I will mention a few of them so that you will get the general idea:

- ❖ **Management by objective**—Each goal that the employee accomplishes is awarded with a certain number of points.

- ❖ **Number of *X***—This can measure many things, such as product defects, document errors, or software bugs.

- ❖ **180/360-degree feedback**—With 180-degree feedback, the employee's direct colleagues and manager provide feedback. With 360-degree feedback, the feedback comes from peers, subordinates, customers, and a manager.

- ❖ **Work quantity**—This can include the number of sales, number of items produced, number of customer support calls taken, and so forth.

Remember that the employee performance measurements you use (also known as "indicators") must be measurable, quantifiable, and adjustable. A popular acronym to help remember this is SMART:

S—Specific

M—Measurable

A—Achievable

R—Realistic

T—Time-framed

One way to know if you have hit on the right indicator is to evaluate if it is a key contributor to the success of the goal. It's important to define how the indicator is measured. There is often more than one way to measure something, which can result in different outputs.

One last piece of advice on indicators...you need to find the Goldilocks zone. Don't use too many, or they are unmanageable. Don't use too few, or your overall results might be skewed.

Track Progress

When you track an employee's progress, it's referred to as performance monitoring. It's important to do this at regular intervals in order to provide coaching or feedback when needed. You can also help the employee deal with roadblocks or prepare "plan B" if a deadline is missed. Additionally, if the business direction changes, you can work with the employee to re-assess or change the goals.

You can obtain performance information by personal observation and talking to others. Just keep in mind that these two methods are considered subjective and can be influenced by the various factors that make up human beings: mood, emotion, point-of-view, personality, and so forth.

Another important activity around performance monitoring is note taking. You need to document all significant episodes, both positive and negative. This helps to support future performance or personnel decisions.

Offer Feedback and Coaching

Just as you regularly monitor employees' performance, you should provide ongoing performance feedback. In fact, one way an organization can drive goal-related performance improvements is to build constructive feedback into its day-to-day activities.

One-on-one sessions for employees demonstrate caring and concern as well as help employees develop good habits. It can help if leaders expand their perceived role as managers of people and work and strive to serve as coaches and mentors to the employees in their department or on their team.

Here are some more tips on providing feedback:

❖ Feedback should be objective, supportive, and delivered with respect.

❖ Deliver feedback when it is most relevant so that the employee can make the necessary changes.

❖ To help make your points clear, use specific examples.

❖ Focus the conversation less on past problems and mistakes and more on future improvements.

❖ Listen to the employee's perspective and incorporate it into future plans, as employees often experience roadblocks a manager may not see.

Provide Performance Reviews

The performance review is the formal confirmation of what has already been discussed with the employee across the previous period. The previous period can refer to the last three months, last six months, or last year, depending on how often you provide employee performance reviews.

Although it's possible that business goals and/or individual goals might change regularly, you should strive to maintain the regular schedule of performance reviews. In this way, it gradually becomes a part of the company's culture and operations.

To help establish a regular schedule, you can sometimes link the performance review with a process, such as month-end close or a quarterly inventory review. You might even be able to pull some indicators (i.e., metrics) from these associated processes.

Give Rewards and Recognition

A rewards program is monetary or at least has a cost to your organization. Although a recognition program might be combined with a rewards program, the recognition itself has no intrinsic value and is intended to provide a psychological benefit to the employee.

Although you might choose to link employees' performance to their salary, before you do this you should ensure your performance management system is in place and being followed and maintained. This ensures that the system is fair and equitable. If this is done right, it can significantly increase job satisfaction. To encourage individual and group performance, consider providing rewards at both of these levels.

Monetary rewards can include bonuses, profit-sharing, and stock options. Although you might think that most employees are motivated by such financial benefits, recent research has proved that a non-financial recognition program is more effective in terms of:

❖ Strengthening teamwork

❖ Improving customer satisfaction

❖ Reinforcing company values and culture

❖ Motivating specific behaviors

The one exception to this was in rewarding increasing sales.

A recognition program needs to be time-sensitive. For example, it makes more sense to acknowledge the employee when the performance being recognized is still fresh in everyone's mind. If an employee consistently deserves recognition, it must be provided in such a way so that it doesn't seem automatic.

Some common recognition "prizes" include the ability to come into work late or leave early, working from home for a day, or taking a long lunch. You could also consider giving the employee their choice in assignments.

Difficulties and Pitfalls

With so many factors in play (especially the fact that people are involved, and people are complicated), it's likely that problems will crop up. I hope you can read this as a watch-out-for section, but if that fails and there are issues, you can always use the information below for troubleshooting.

Processes That Are Poorly Designed or Managed

From the beginning, ensure that each component of the performance management system adds value to your organization. Otherwise, you will experience problems with resistance, non-participation, lack of employee engagement, or worse.

Here's a short checklist:

_____ Are individual goals aligned with the business strategy?

_____ Do employees understand the organization's overall performance goals and how they individually contribute to it?

_____ Is there a clear differentiation between top performers and underperformers in regard to performance ratings, rewards, recognition, opportunities, and compensation?

_____ Are you holding employee appraisals more than once per year? (An annual process will not adequately alert managers to problems in a timely manner.)

_____ Is performance information available and easy for employees to access?

_____ Are you properly documenting all performance-related events and discussions?

_____ Are goals, deadlines, and other targets meaningful and attainable? This applies to individuals, teams, departments, and the organization.

Complex or Time-Consuming Processes

The overall system must be efficient and as simple as possible, but still provide value. You can use scheduling tools with automated reminders to help the system stay on track.

Lack of Management Understanding or Support

If your company's leaders and/or management don't understand why you need a performance management system or they don't know how it works, you will end up with a host of problems like:

❖ Incomplete or late appraisals

❖ Avoidance of performance feedback

❖ Employee mistrust and resistance

❖ Unhelpful feedback on employee performance

Management support is therefore a crucial element in the success of your performance management system. This consists of both verbal support and actionable support. Regarding the latter, management must also participate on both ends of the process – as reviewer and reviewee.

Along those lines, managers need to be visible on a daily basis, which provides these benefits:

❖ Make performance monitoring a daily habit

❖ Send the right message to employees

❖ Be available as a role model and to identify improvements and solve problems

An Unsupportive Culture

If things aren't going well with your performance management system and it's difficult to put your finger on the exact reason, it could be your culture. Ask yourself if the workplace truly has an atmosphere that supports the process. Does the culture support open and honest communication, or are employees fearful and avoidant after making mistakes? If you answered "no" to either of these questions, you should revisit Chapter 5, "Become

Culturally Aware," and deeply consider the values that you have identified as being important to your organization.

Confusing the Indicator with the Goal

This can occur if employees are only working to specific targets without valuing their work or a concern for quality. Employees must understand the link between the results on the company's balance sheet and their own individual goals.

Wrong Performance Indicators and/or Goals

The employee performance indicators you use must be key contributors to the success of the employee's goal. Make sure that you are not inadvertently promoting a goal that is contrary to your culture or values (for example, emphasizing *quantity* output when *quality* is an important value).

In addition, the targets the employee must reach should be not too easy and not too hard. Set a goal that requires the employee to stretch their abilities, intelligence, skills, etc., but one that is not out of reach.

Lack of Communication

Make sure the feedback loop isn't broken. Managers or team leads must regularly monitor performance and provide feedback, mentoring, or coaching. In addition, employees must be able to understand the feedback and act on it so as to illustrate performance improvements.

Chapter Summary

Now that we've finished this chapter, I hope you understand why it's important for your organization to have a performance management system and the benefits you can recognize from having one. It enables you to make better personnel decisions, communicates expectations about job performance, rewards the highest performers, and links strategic vision and goals to individual employee performance. It's also helps you evaluate the skills you currently have and prepare for future goals and challenges.

All of the components of a performance management system are equally important, and I believe that if one isn't present or isn't working properly, the entire system will suffer. Remember, there are seven components:

- ❖ Plan

- ❖ Goals

- ❖ Metrics

- ❖ Monitoring

- ❖ Feedback

- ❖ Reviews

- ❖ Rewards

If you run into trouble, revisit the basics in this chapter and try to identify where things are falling flat. Experiencing issues from time to time is normal and probably just indicates that you need to tweak one or more areas.

What is the makeup of a successful salesperson?

SCOTT LEESE

In general, great salespeople are good listeners, optimistic thinkers, highly competitive and motivated, and are always looking to learn and improve.

RICHARD HARRIS

Resilience and empathy. It takes resilience to learn the new craft, and it takes empathy to learn to keep your own mouth shut. If they can prove this to me, then I can teach them the rest.

SAMAR BIRWADKER

Innovator. Drive. Maverick. Go getter. These are a few of the personas that Good&Co identified as people who are self-driven motivators, and who can dust themselves off when they get knocked down. They're dynamic, creative, and curious, making them ambitious salespeople.

KYLE PORTER

Same as the sales manager - relentlessly driven to serve others.

Chapter 9 – Build a Winning Sales Team

One of the most important aspects of scaling your business is hiring for sales and building a strong sales team. Finding the right people for a sales position is doubly important; if you make a hiring mistake, not only do you have a poor employee who is affecting morale, you have someone who isn't selling!

According to the results of a 2015 - 2016 survey by DePaul University, the turnover for sales positions averages about 26%, with the cost per turnover approximately $97,690. Can your business afford that? Hiring and then having to fire someone in sales (or having them quit) can be a serious blow if you're trying to scale up. Therefore, when it comes to interviewing and hiring for sales positions, be extra careful and attentive.

The overall goal in hiring for sales is to create a sales team that can create scalable, predictable revenue growth. It's entirely possible to build such a team, but if you try to just wing it, you'll quickly realize that when it comes to sales teams, there are too many "moving parts" to make winging it worthwhile. By sticking to an overall process, you'll be able to avoid a lot of rookie mistakes, which will save you time, money, and aggravation.

At the same time, as you work through the process of hiring, building, and organizing your sales team, you should regularly review what is working and what is not and be open to change. Just ensure sure the changes you make are backed up by actual data whenever possible. Try to avoid relying entirely on those "gut feelings," or you'll find yourself back to winging it again!

Structure the Sales Team

You may be years away from having an actual sales floor teeming with staff, but you should still put some thought now into how you'll organization the sales department. You'll need to keep that in mind when evaluating which candidates are the right fit for what you envision.

Here I'll go over the most common types of structure for a sales department, but there are probably many more configurations that borrow from these concepts:

All-In-One Sales Rep

Sales reps manage their own sales process from beginning to end. Proponents of this structure like its simplicity and competitive nature. Critics say that it's difficult to communicate a consistent product message across clients, as sales reps have their own way of doing their job. Also, you can imagine how difficult it might be for a new salesperson to adjust to this atmosphere. In this world of sink-or-swim, many will sink.

Assembly Line Sales

This might sound rather derogatory, but it's not meant to be that way. It just seems like the best way to explain a sales department in which each employee has a specialty that mirrors a stage of the sales process: lead generation, sales development, closing, and client relationship management. The assembly line makes it easy to spot bottlenecks and react accordingly. I go into a bit more detail in the next section, "SDR Versus Account Executives."

Sales Pod

A sales pod takes the Assembly Line concept a step further. Each pod has its own lead generation, sales development, etc. Several pods make up the sales organization. Those who like this structure praise the adaptability of the pods and how pod members motivate and encourage each other.

If you're looking for a downside, it could be that pod members give each other too much slack, and the sales effort becomes too laid-back. And if you're just starting out with one or two sales employees, this type of structure wouldn't work.

Build a Sales Playbook

Your sales staff is going to need structure and guidance for how they actual bring in leads and close deals. At the very least, you should have a sales playbook, which includes a sales pitch, methods for handling objections, and competitive advantages. Other types of documents that are helpful for new salespeople are:

❖ Call review checklist

❖ Call scripts

❖ Email templates

❖ Multi-week onboarding schedule

❖ Sales process

Consider these as "living documents" that need frequent updating (weekly or monthly). Thanks to the growing availability of sales management software, keeping track of this material and sharing it with the sales team easier than it used to be.

A customer relationship management (CRM) system is the foundation on which a great sales organization rests. The CRM software might already include the ability to create and manage email templates; if not, you might be able to use an "add-on" software to get this feature. Other helpful CRM or sales software features include the ability to upload sales messaging and marketing assets into the shared playbook.

It's extremely useful for everyone on the sales team to see top-performing email templates, get notified when a new template is available, or see the email template that helped seal the deal.

Another useful sales tool is the ability to use analytics to determine which sales messages, collateral, and strategies help book more meetings, close deals, and grow accounts.

Determine Sales Territories

Another consideration is how you'll divide the sales leads – that is, the sales territories. While some companies use geographical territories or alphabetical-by-name structure, that doesn't always work, especially for certain product types or global products. Other ways to divide sales territory are:

❖ Buying power

❖ Company size

❖ Inbound and outbound

❖ Industry type

Some companies even choose to pool all the leads together, allowing sales reps to pull from the pool and build a call list. This enables the reps to focus on their specialties and take advantage of any previous experience or industry knowledge.

How to Hire for Sales

When you hire for sales, first determine and document the criteria you're looking for. This makes it possible to have a repeatable process for finding a successful sales person. As you hire and learn from your experiences, you'll likely need to adjust what criteria has worked and what hasn't.

Some traits to look in job candidates are prior success, intelligence, work ethic, and coachability. If your job prospect has prior sales experience, you should prefer those who have been able to sell based on value and not price.

If you're just starting out with a sales team, it's best to start with someone who has sales development experience. Sales development reps (also known as SDRs) already have the foundation for handling buyers' objections, and they can articulate the value of the product/service they are selling.

SDR Versus Account Executives: What You Need to Know

Nowadays, a lot of businesses have separated their sales departments into areas of specialization – SDRs and account executives. The SDR role focuses on finding prospects who are a good fit for your product. The account executive role concentrates on closing the deal.

Here's a quick summary of the differences:

Sales Development Representative	Account Executive
Also referred to as *business development reps* (BDRs) or *inside sales reps*.	Also referred to as *sales reps* or *salespeople*.
Main job responsibilities include finding leads, making sure they are a good prospect (i.e., qualifying the lead), and tracking down their contact information.	Main job responsibilities are to demonstrate or present the product, discover the prospect's pain points, and address them.
Reaches out with phone and email. Use software prospecting tools to store and track lead information.	Share value proposition and product details as well as negotiate terms.
Quotas based on the number of qualified demos or appointments scheduled.	Quota based on the number of closed deals.

One of the reasons why specializing works so well in sales is that it's difficult to find one person who can do all of the above tasks well. It's more realistic and easier to find job candidates who are good at either one or the other of these roles.

Traits You Need to Look For

Whether you're looking for help in qualifying and finding leads or someone with demonstrated experience in closing sales, keep in mind that many sales skills and techniques can be taught, but it is difficult to teach the inherent character traits of persistence and intelligence.

Look for someone with an entrepreneurial spirit like your own who's competitive and has a high tolerance for rejection. At the same time, they should be coachable, have compassion, and great communication skills.

By the way, "communication skills" don't mean just talking. Someone who has developed the habit of listening is going to be easier to train than a talker. And someone who is a listener is going to be able to respond to prospects needs much more accurately.

If you want to raise the bar extra high, you can also look for these traits:

❖ Charisma

❖ Shamelessness

❖ Detail oriented

❖ Critical thinker

Of course, you also want someone with a work ethic... one that's almost as strong as your own.

In general, using Craigslist or any of the other job posting boards is going to take a lot of time. Better to use your own network or look to businesses in your market that are a couple of years ahead of you in development.

Even if you aren't looking to hire immediately, get in the habit of jotting down the names of "people with potential" whom you meet in both your social and business life. LinkedIn is great for initiating these types of connections.

How to Conduct the Interview

Phone interviews are viewed with favor by human resources and hiring managers because they think of them as a time saver. However, you might want to rethink this practice when you consider that:

❖ You can schedule an in-person interview to last the same amount of time as a phone interview.

❖ You can pick up on certain subtleties, such as demeanor and appearance, when you meet someone in person for the first time. This kind of non-verbal information is almost impossible to pick up from a phone interview.

❖ Even if the in-person interview is a let-down, you can at least form a network connection with that person. This is more difficult and awkward to do after a non-inspiring telephone interview.

Of course, no interview is complete without questions. Although you might pride yourself on your ability to interview by the seat of your pants, I don't recommend you do this. A set of questions helps to structure the overall interview and gets the conversation flowing. After some initial chit-chat, the goal is to ask questions and be on the look-out for thoughtful answers that illustrate specific traits.

Sales Assessments

If you're not confident of your ability to hire a person with innate sales talent, you can use pre-employment assessment testing. Various online tools are available in this arena, but a well-known tool for sales hiring is the Sales Aptitude Questionnaire (APQ) from Asher Strategies.

You can use the APQ to gauge sales reps on some of the traits mentioned above as well as other traits, such as time management and self-reliance.

Some software-based sales assessment tools let you manage the sales candidates' tests and pertinent information from a dashboard. The dashboard also lets you know when the candidate has completed the test. The candidate's test score should be used in combination with a series of interview questions the company provides based on the results of the assessment.

Another method of assessment for a candidate is a writing test. Composing an email message to a prospect reveals not only how this potential salesperson would represent your company, but also how the person thinks.

Besides looking over the grammar and readability, pay attention to the information included in the email. This is particularly important if the candidate claims to have prior sales or business experience.

Consider Hiring Two Sales Reps at Once

If the budget allows it, think about hiring for two sales positions instead of just one. Some benefits of this include:

❖ Having the advantages of an instant team, such as co-worker competition and support

❖ Relying less on one person's performance

❖ Obtaining more data to analyze sales results, determine time to ramp up, and so forth

Tied into this consideration is the length of your product's sales cycle. Does it take just a few phone calls to close the deal, or is developing the client/sales relationship a 6- to 8-month wooing period? Answering that question can also help you determine the character traits and experience necessary to run your company's sales.

About Paying Your Salespeople

Salespeople like to get paid. Do yourself and your organization a favor and keep the sales compensation plan simple, especially in the beginning.

First, determine the sales rep's entire compensation amount. To determine the split between base pay and variable pay (commission and bonuses), refer again to your product's sales cycle. Shorter sales cycles should have a smaller percentage of base pay relative to the total compensation. If your product has a long sales cycle, your sales staff should have a higher percentage of base bay. Lastly, always make sure to create a tiered sales compensation program that has rich accelerators in place when your sales team exceeds goals.

Onboarding, Training, and Ongoing Learning

Keeping in mind what I went over in Chapter 7, "Invest in Your People," you need to train your sales people consistently. That's why I recommend you document your company procedures and assemble a sales playbook.

If possible, give the new employee the time and space to work with your product the same way a client would. For example, if you sell software that helps small businesses evaluate their net worth, have the new employee create a fake company and use the software. Short of actually observing a customer as they are using your product, that is the best way to familiarize new employees with your product. Hands-on knowledge is more easily remembered that just reading or hearing about it.

Make sure new employees understand the acronyms and glossary of the terms you use at your business, especially those used within the sales department. Give them either an online or paper resource for this type of information so they can refer back to it often. Don't be shy about testing new employees on their product and terminology knowledge before they start performing their day-to-day activities.

Another important aspect of sales, especially for account executives, is to learn how to think quickly on their feet. Some people are just naturally good at this, but others need practice.

New employees will learn best by first watching, then doing. Some of your more experienced sales staff may enjoy helping out in this way. You'll need to get new employees comfortable with call scripts, handling objections, and performing demos. Even SDRs need to understand how to take a conversation into a more favorable direction.

Enhance the Sales Team Culture

After you hire one or more people for sales, don't hand off the baton! Your work isn't done. As the head of the business, it's your responsibility to see that sales, whether it's a single sales employee or a team, starts off on the right foot with an appropriately motivating and supporting culture. I've been over culture thoroughly in Chapter 5, so I won't go over that again, but I do want to mention some important aspects of sales culture.

The frequent rejections that sales employees receive need to be balanced with an energetic, motivational sales culture. Entire books and blogs are devoted to creating and maintaining a positive sales culture, so those are a good place to start.

You'll need to put your own twist on ideas to make them your own and to seem genuine, not "tacked on." Even if you're just starting out sales with a single SDR, you can generate excitement throughout the company by "ringing the bell" or indulging in an impromptu, company-wide celebration.

Technology can also help create a positive sales culture, though in a subtler way. You can use sales management software to help motivate and engage your sales staff using individual and team "scorecards" displayed on a large monitor screen.

Another important aspect of sales culture is team building, where everyone steps away from their desk to enjoy each other's company. Try to vary the activities or the get-togethers to accommodate employees across different age groups and with different personality types.

It's better if these get-togethers happen naturally, but if they don't, you need to lead the way. Not everyone is going to end up best friends, but within a great team, individuals should demonstrate respect and some enjoyment in each other's company.

Keep Communication Flowing and Easily Accessible

You've probably heard the saying, "Everyone is in sales." This is most applicable when your business is a startup or very small. If that's your situation, everyone in your company needs to be aware of and fulfill the role of sales when the opportunity presents itself.

If you'll remember, I mentioned making the sales- and company-specific acronyms and glossary available for new sales employees. I want to suggest you make this information available to others in your company. It's important for *everyone* in the company, whether they are HR, finance, or production, to be fluent in the sales language.

Within the sales department, you should have a plan for how you will keep everyone aligned and sharing the same language. Regular check-in meetings are one way to achieve this. You can ask questions and gather feedback as well as solicit questions and ideas. When sales people share what works for them, it adds to the positive energy in sales and encourages even more creative solutions.

You can also use technology to disseminate news and information. As I mentioned earlier, software enables people to share the same email templates and call scripts. You can also use podcast technology or online learning to teach and coach your sales players. While it's assumed that modern sales departments use a CRM system to track appointments, opportunities, and notes about potential customer conversations, you can also find features that support:

❖ Tracking and displaying suggested changes to sales documents

❖ Discussing sales documents and their changes online

If everyone in the sales department is committed to transparency and communication, the team can only grow stronger through shared knowledge. You'll also avoid the common frustration that employees experience in not knowing "what's going on."

Collaborate with Other Departments

Here's an interesting tidbit… businesses that have a highly aligned sales and marketing departments achieve 208% higher revenue than those teams without alignment. If you'd like to enjoy some extra revenue through a better relationship between sales and marketing, you first need to understand each other's roles and processes. Furthermore, you must communicate this commitment to your sales team members.

One way to do this is to encourage your sales staff to set aside time regularly – perhaps weekly or monthly – to spend with the marketing team. The best way to learn and improve is to express interest and curiosity about how marketing works and vice versa.

You could also hold meetings between the two groups at lesser intervals, say once per quarter. These meetings would have a definite agenda based on working toward the sale lead and revenue goals, pinning down information such as:

❖ Sources that drive the most traffic to the website

❖ Content or emails that produce the most leads and conversions

❖ Upcoming campaigns or content pieces

All communication between the two areas should be respectful. Blaming and complaining aren't productive. Focus on the results you have seen. Ask if there are suggestions for improvement. In particular, make sure (again) that you are speaking the same language when you talk about the company, marketing, and sales processes. For example:

❖ Qualifying a lead in sales versus qualifying a lead in marketing

❖ Adding opportunities to the pipeline in the same way

❖ Following the same process for onboarding new clients and/or renewal clients

Difficulties and Pitfalls

In this chapter, I've tried to point out the actions you can take to avoid making mistakes when hiring for and growing your sales personnel. However, there are a few more things I'd like to address before wrapping it all up.

Hiring for Sales Too Early

Just because you have found a product-market fit doesn't mean you should go out and hire five sales employees. As the founder of the company, you should have a proven track record of being able to sell the product yourself. Only after you have a predictable and repeatable process (remember the sales playbook?) should you consider hiring for sales.

If you're not sure the time is right, try figuring it out from the bottom of the funnel:

1. Define how much revenue you need to generate.
2. Identify how many deals you need to generate that revenue.
3. Determine how many emails, calls, and demos need to take place to close those deals.

If you don't have the headcount to take care of those emails, calls, and demos, then it's time to hire.

Can't Find the Goldilocks Zone

Remember that as you and the sales team strive to reach quotas, you are also scaling your company for growth. If you expend all of your energy on driving sales to meet quotas, what will happen when it's time to hire again to meet the incoming sales demand? As you work with your sales team, you need to place an emphasis on identifying and coaching future sales leaders.

Your top sales talent can each train several more top-performing employees. I've mentioned it before, but I'll say it again here: it's so much better to hire from within.

At the same time, you need to avoid over-focusing on growing the number of employees you have. What can happen in this situation is that the sales team is overwhelmed with having to constantly train new employees, and that leads to underperformance.

Not Investing in Top-Notch Technology Tools

Don't skimp on purchasing software licenses or on the quality of the software you purchase. That doesn't mean you have to sign up for the most expensive (and popular) sales tool on the market but avoid those on the lower end of the pricing scale. You don't want your sales team dealing with buggy software or getting bogged down with manual processes that should be handled by the software. You also don't want to risk losing your prospect and customer data to a fly-by-night company.

You should also avoid forcing your sales team to use software that doesn't quite work for them. Even if the software works well for your leadership team or used to work when you were a smaller company, your sales people need all the tools possible to streamline their workflow and data entry.

Underpaying the Sales Staff

I would hope that you wouldn't pay under the average yearly salary for any of your job positions, but you especially don't want to do this with your sales employees. In addition to figuring out the commission package, make sure you've researched an average base pay. For more information, refer back to the "About Paying Your Salespeople" section.

Getting Complacent

Even when things are going well, you must always be on the lookout for areas of improvement. This can be anything from an employee who needs individual coaching to testing the results of two different email templates. Don't be afraid to ask, "What if…?" or any other questions that could lead to a more efficient and effective sales workflow.

Chapter Summary

This is one of the longer chapters I've written, and for good reason. As I wrote earlier, a successful sales team has a lot of moving parts. From the high-level aspects of creating a positive sales culture to the low-level details of editing templates, there is no part of sales that shouldn't receive your close attention or scrutiny.

If it helps, think of the sales team as a house. Your sales playbook is what you live in. The sales team members are its residents. You don't want just anyone to move in, so you screen job candidates carefully. When a new employee does move in, you show them around and get them familiar with how things are done (onboarding and training). The sales culture is the overall mood and atmosphere of the team members.

Every business is different, and you may find that for some areas, you need to go your own way or tweak some of the components or processes to keep things moving along. As long as you understand the importance of each of these sales areas, I think it's perfectly fine to experiment. Just remember to support your different activities with real data to see if it's working!

What bad recommendations have you heard along the years on growing a business?

MIKITA MIKADO

The worst advice was not to do it in the first place.

BOB MARSH

Hire people to grow faster, especially in the early days. As a first-time founder and CEO, I heard this from too many people and shouldn't have listened. We spent way too much money and time throwing more bodies at processes and product that just weren't ready. In particular, we hired a VP of Sales way too early. As someone with years of sales and sales leadership experience myself, I should have run our sales team for much longer so that as CEO I could remain very close to the process and the people. We absolutely would have grown faster had we done this and not burned so much money to get there.

Chapter 10 – The Economics of a Sale – Get It Right!

While most of my information up to this point can be applied to any type of business, the nature of what I'm going to discuss in this chapter requires me to focus on a specific industry – SaaS (Software as a Service). It can also apply to ecommerce. Just keep that in mind if your business doesn't fall into either of those areas. You will still be able to get the gist of what I'm saying, but you may have to change out some of the metrics I mention for ones that are more appropriate to your industry.

Providing software to customers using the SaaS business model is different than selling other products. For SaaS, the emphasis is on creating recurring and consistent revenue via subscriptions, upsells, seat expansion, and so forth. If you can accomplish this on a small scale and then repeat it as you keep growing, as long as you keep your customer acquisition cost in line, you have the model for a successful and profitable business.

Timing is important as you are scaling your business. If you find what you think is a great product-market fit and rush to hire too many sales employees, you may find yourself short of cash just when you most need it. On the other hand, if you don't grab as much market share as possible as you're growing (particularly if you have a new or emerging SaaS product), you'll always be playing "catch up" with your competitors.

Because timing is so important, in order to grow at a comfortable pace, you need to recognize when you have a scalable sales model that can be repeated over and over again. This chapter can help you understand how to evaluate the effectiveness of your sales and marketing in converting prospects into customers. You don't want to accelerate your company's growth before understanding the components that help drive that growth.

What Is Sales Efficiency and Why Is It Important?

Sales efficiency is a measurement of how productive a company's sales department is. In the SaaS industry, the formula used to calculate sales efficiency is referred to as the *Magic Number*. When a company is scaling, its sales efficiency is an important indicator of its current state of health. This number tells you if you'll generate enough revenue to recoup what you have expended in acquiring customers. (More on that later.)

You can also use sales efficiency to make short-, medium- and long-term financial plans. (For example, should you hire more sales employees? If so, how many?) If your sales efficiency metric isn't good, you can make corrections in your strategy or processes.

Another reason why it's important to know your sales efficiency is that it can help you find your way through a difficult period many SaaS companies experience. When scaling, you can lose money faster than you are growing because of the costs incurred in hiring new sales employees. It can take many months to make back this "investment" in sales, so knowing your sales efficiency can help you determine how long that losing period will last. Being able to monitor your sales efficiency will help you grow as quickly as possible, but without overextending your resources.

Sales efficiency is one of the numbers that investors use to compare startups and scaling companies across many industries and sectors. If necessary, you can use the sales efficiency measurement to help obtain additional financing or investors. It's also possible to use it as a tool to see how your company compares to its competitors (if this information is available).

Speaking of competitors, one of the most important aspects of scaling your business is related to market share. If you have a new or different kind of product and you grab the majority of customers before more competitors emerge or catch up to you, it's likely that you will remain a market leader. This is because you create a positive cycle. Prospects naturally prefer to buy from the leader in the marketplace, and you're likely to get more good press and attention because you're the leader, and so forth.

How to Calculate Your Sales Efficiency

As you can imagine, several different methods exist for calculating sales efficiency. The method I use for this chapter is the one commonly used for SaaS or ecommerce companies. If you have a business type other than these two, you may need to make some adjustments for your calculations.

Customer Acquisition Cost (CAC)

One of the first numbers you need to figure out is your *customer acquisition cost*. This is the cost to acquire a single customer. You can calculate CAC by dividing your marketing and sales cost by the number of deals closed:

```
Marketing and Sales Cost / Number of Deals Closed
```

Lifetime Value (LTV)

The next important number to determine is the *lifetime value* of a single customer. This is the revenue you expect to generate from a single customer over the lifetime of the account with your business. You can calculate LTV by multiplying together these three metrics:

```
       Gross Margin % * Monthly Churn % *
  Average Amount Each Customer Spends Per Month
```

The LTV/CAC Ratio

Once you have the CAC and LTV calculated, divide LTV by CAC to get your sales efficiency:

```
LTV / CAC
```

The "ideal" sales efficiency number is 3... as in your customers contribute three times more value than it cost to acquire them.

If this number is below 2, stop spending money on sales right now. Look for ways to either improve sales efficiency, improve your product's staying power, or both.

The CAC Payback

Another important metric is how long it takes your business to earn back what it has invested in CAC. You can think of this as the breakeven point. One reason this is important is that it helps you determine how much cash you'll need to not only stay alive, but also to keep growing. The shorter this period is, the faster you can get your company to the point of being profitable.

Here is the formula for calculating CAC Payback:

$$(CAC \ / \ ARPU) \ * \ Gross \ Margin \ \%$$

First divide CAC by the ARPU (Average Revenue Per User), then multiply that by the Gross Margin Percent. Note that ARPU is the *monthly* revenue per customer/user.

The result is the number of months it takes to payback your customer acquisition cost. You need to get this number to be less than 12 months.

Factors to Consider

Below I've summarized information about some of the factors that can impact LTV and CAC. This is obviously a deep topic, so if you get curious or excited about something I've mentioned below, you'll definitely want to dig deeper with more research.

The Sales Organization

You can optimize sales efficiency by reviewing these areas of your sales organization:

❖ Conversion funnels

❖ Cross-sells, seat expansion, and upsell strategy

❖ Incentives

❖ Lead sources

❖ Partnership strategy

❖ Product expansion

❖ Sales hiring

❖ Sales targets/quotas

❖ Vertical focus

One of the key factors that affects the CAC is how much of the human sales touch is needed in order to convert a lead into a sale. Those businesses that have a "touchless" conversion" obviously have awesome sales efficiency. This may not be completely doable for your company, but there might be some areas that can be automated to reduce the cost of human labor.

The sales funnel is another place that is very important to optimize. For example, if you can convert twice as many leads, you can lower the CAC by half.

If you can optimize your sales funnel, then the more leads you drive into the funnel via your marketing program, the better. Of course, you need to keep a close eye on marketing costs to make sure they're effective and monitored closely to keep the overall company-level LTV/CAC in a healthy operating zone.

Make sure you have set the sales quotas at a challenging (but not impossible) level. New sales employees should receive the appropriate level of training, while existing sales employees can be encouraged in performance with coaching and mentoring.

The Customer Relationship

Determining your company's most profitable customers, channels, and location and then focusing marketing and sales efforts only in that direction will lower customer acquisition cost (CAC). Especially as a SaaS company, you can increase customer value by establishing strong relationships with them. This, along with strong customer training (or retraining) programs, can help lower churn.

Another aspect related to customers, though technically not customer acquisition cost, is customer onboarding and service cost. This falls under the cost of goods sold (COGS), which affects your gross margin.

The Churn Rate

You may remember seeing the churn rate (or just "churn") as part of the calculation of lifetime value (LTV):

```
   Gross Margin % * Monthly Churn % *
Average Amount Each Customer Spends Per Month
```

The churn rate is the percentage of customers who decide not to renew their service with your business. You can look into lowering your churn rate in an effort to increase the LTV, which then increases your sales efficiency.

If you are unable to lower your churn (don't feel badly, it happens to the best of companies), it helps if your sales people can increase the revenue per customer over time. This can be accomplished through upselling, cross selling, and so forth. In this way, you can offset some of the lost revenue from churn.

Customer Segmentation

Another helpful way to track your sales efficiency is by customer segmentation. By tracking the LTC/CAC Ratio and the CAC Payback for each segment, you have a level of detail that makes it easier to evaluate the effects of your sales efforts (funnel, campaigns, quotas, etc.).

For example, let's say you have three customer segments, and you discover that one segment has higher CAC than your other two segments. You can look at those other two segments and do more digging to find out why they are more successful and attempt to reproduce that effect on the segment with higher CAC.

Difficulties and Pitfalls

As I mentioned earlier, this is a deep topic, so don't get discouraged if you run into problems. I've gone over a few of them in this section.

If You Have "Bad" Numbers

If you've discovered that your LTV/CAC ratio is less than two or your CAC Payback is more than 12 months, it's not a disaster. It could be that you are just not scaling as fast as you would like. If you believe that's the case, stop hiring sales people until your CAC has been paid back.

Cash Dribbles Instead of Flows

A SaaS business can be tricky because there is such a high upfront cost in acquiring a customer. Although you might be getting those customers left and right, the cash that's coming in is in smaller amounts over a longer period of time.

One solution is to offer longer term contracts to customers that include an advance payment. Offering a discount for customers who sign up for a longer period of time can help to sweeten the deal.

If you infuse your organization with more cash through the advance payments, you will reach your CAC Payback point more quickly and avoid having to obtain financing to tide you over.

Marketing Leads Plateau

It's not unusual for your normal "go to" lead generation programs (for example, Pay-Per-Click) to plateau over time. You might find that they aren't producing as many leads even as you are spending the same amount as always. This is, of course, a problem because it slows down the rate at which leads are entering your sales funnel.

What most businesses end up doing is layering another marketing program on top of the existing one in order to keep growing at a steady rate.

You can also look into implementing or improving your *inbound marketing* techniques, which is a way of bringing customers to you by providing better content on the web (such as white papers, case studies, blog posts, etc.). Depending on your SaaS product, your inbound marketing may lead to some "touchless conversions" that are very good for your LTV/CAC Ratio.

If you cannot increase the number of leads entering your sales funnel, you may have to adjust your sales hiring accordingly.

It's All So Confusing/Difficult/Overwhelming!

I don't blame you if you find this information rather overwhelming. Not all of us enjoy digging into the numbers side of our business, so if this is something you think you'll hate doing, I recommend you hire someone, perhaps as a freelancer, to help set this up for you. Or you may have an enterprising employee who has an aptitude and interest in running the numbers.

One thing I can recommend is to take a high-level view of this at first to get the hang of it. For example, instead of segmenting your customers and then looking at the LTV/CAC Ratio of each, calculate it for all of your customers regardless of segment or campaign. As you get more comfortable, you can start looking at your various customer segments or the effect of different marketing programs.

Chapter Summary

I hope this chapter has pointed you in the right direction to know the current state of your sales efficiency. If your LTV/CAC Ratio isn't good, at least you have the information and knowledge to dig deeper and find out why. The CAC Payback is another indicator that can be reassuring and empowering as you deal with the negative numbers that often result from scaling your company.

Understanding LTV, CAC, and the factors that affect them can also help you remain objective about where you need to focus your energy and resources. Remember to seek out assistance if you think it's going to be difficult to regularly monitor your sales efficiency.

Chapter 11 – Unite Your Sales Force Through Revenue Operations

In the past 15 years, increasingly affluent societies have been using technology for more than just communication and entertainment. Technology is now a tool to order and deliver into our homes clothes, food, household goods, and even auto parts.

The amount of data collected from these transactions has swelled, giving companies much better insight into what drives their customers' purchasing decisions. What does that mean for Marketing, Sales, and Customer Success departments? Data. Lots and lots of data.

Someone needs to manage all of this data, and it usually has fallen onto the lap of the IT department (it's technology, right?) or a Data Team. The tasks were to get the data, manipulate the data, and manage the data. The purpose? To use the data to better understand, attract, and woo customers.

While all of this was happening, the SaaS concept was also growing. This enabled software companies to produce and deliver software products to consumers more efficiently and profitably than the previous on-premise software installation business model. Not coincidentally, the number of software products created to help manage all of the consumer data has virtually exploded on the landscape.

Out of all this has evolved a hybrid type of operations team to help manage the data and the software tools. But they can even do much more than that.

By analyzing the data, they can provide invaluable assistance to a company's leadership team. For that reason, they've been given the impressive name of "Revenue Operations."

What Is Revenue Operations?

When you think about it, *revenue* is the link that binds together all areas of a business. Also referred to as Sales Ops, Revenue Operations (Rev Ops) can bridge the gap between the leadership's go-to-market strategy and the sales team's tactics.

If you can imagine the sales funnel:

❖ Marketing is at the top of the funnel, sending leads to Sales.

❖ Sales is in the middle of the funnel, closing the deals.

❖ Customer Success is at the bottom of the funnel, working to retain and further monetize the customer.

Well, Rev Ops is all over that funnel, helping each of these areas perform their job to the best of their abilities.

What Does Rev Ops Do?

Rev Ops is about providing the tools, insights, and processes to Marketing, Sales, and Customer Success (MSCS). Below are the activities and areas that Rev Ops is involved in:

❖ *Analysis*—Interpreting the data, such as conversion rates and providing recommendations to optimize the customer life cycle.

❖ *Tools*—Researching, installing, and maintaining the software used by MSCS as well as collecting the data that populates the software. Rev Ops may need to do research and show the potential return on investment in order to justify the cost of new tools. This area of responsibility includes creating reports and maintaining the CRM software.

❖ *Processes*—Developing, managing, and optimizing the key MCSC processes based on the high-level strategy and vision. Most important among these are the sales stages that the customer moves through in the customer lifecycle.

Another important task for Rev Ops is to create one or more buyer personas and ensure they are in agreement with the actual sales process. They're also the troubleshooters for MSCS, removing any obstacles that affect the sales process.

Benefits of a Rev Ops Team

A Revenue Operations team can remove duplication of roles, make the best use of the available technology, and free up time for your marketing and sales specialists. But wait… there's more! (I've always wanted to say that.)

A Resource Focused on Interpreting Data

Using what they know (from past data, current trends, and MSCS insights), Rev Ops can provide essential information that leaders need to set challenging – yet achievable – strategic goals.

Rev Ops can also remain vigilant about the current sales performance and warn them about any possible problems. If necessary, Rev Ops can also look to past sales performance to help determine how a goal was missed and how to correct for the future.

Strategic Alignment of Business Processes

One of Revenue Operations' main responsibilities is to understand the high-level, go-to-market strategy created by your company's leaders and devise the sales processes that will fulfill the strategic goals. If Rev Ops can do this, and these sales activities are repeatable and scalable, then there's a strong likelihood you can meet those goals.

Bridges Communication Gaps

Rev Ops is the natural choice to help Marketing, Sales, and Customer Success communicate better among themselves. This is particularly important when all departments need to agree on metrics. As Rev Ops is already working closely with upper management in regard to the go-to-market strategy, they can also bridge communication gaps with the Finance and Product teams.

Simplifies Tasks and Improves Efficiency

By looking for and removing obstacles from the customer lifecycle, Rev Ops enables MSCS to move faster. As mentioned earlier, Rev Ops is concerned with the sales processes that drive revenue, so they work to tweak and improve these processes. If you improve efficiency, there's the potential to hire more sales employees to fuel faster scaling. Rev Ops can help with that as well by reducing the ramp up time for new hires and shortening the CAC Payback period (covered in Chapter 10).

Increase Revenue

By focusing on the operational and technical tasks for MSCS, these revenue-driving departments are free to focus on generating leads, closing deals, and developing accounts. MSCS becomes more efficient, thus increasing revenue.

Scale Faster

With Rev Ops improving the value and volume of leads, the MSCS teams can increase their pace and conversion rates. This is especially true if Rev Ops focuses on prospects with the highest value and lowest amount of churn. You'll expand your customer base faster and increase revenue.

Because Rev Ops is providing a source of consistent and accurate measurements, you can confidently invest in new markets, new employees, or new strategies. Even better, based on these metrics, you can quickly tell what is working and what is not.

Adjust Better to Changes

Rev Ops is invaluable during times of transition, such as when you're implementing important new software, restructuring territories, or tweaking the compensation model. They can serve as the project manager in these instances to provide communication, training, and troubleshooting, so you will avoid lengthy downtime or lost deals.

The Problem with Traditional Marketing and Sales Departments

It's hard to believe, but the "old days" of marketing and sales are really only about 20 years behind us. In this section, I want to explain how and why the traditional methods for informing customers and selling to them have changed. It will help you better understand why having a Rev Ops team is so crucial for scaling your company.

Shopping Behaviors Are Different

The technology for ecommerce has evolved rapidly in the past 20 years, fueled by consumers' demand for a more convenient way to shop and buy. While software and technology companies have grown in order to support these activities, the traditional methods of marketing and sales have been somewhat slower to respond.

In the "old days," it was all about reaching consumers through advertising (via newspapers, magazines, radio, and TV). When a customer walked into a store, the sales people on the floor were the ones to provide information about the product or service.

The birth of the Internet and ecommerce hasn't wiped out the need for MSCS, but MSCS has had to change how it reaches out to and interacted with customers. Thanks to information being easily available online, most consumers prefer to do their own product research. They do this by reading product reviews online, watching video testimonials, chatting online with customer service reps, and so forth.

Although some marketers persist in telemarketing, the number of buyers who purchase through a conversation over the phone is very small (although there must be some or the telemarketers wouldn't keep calling!). We still get "junk mail" in our mailbox, of course, but again, consumers who have had good online ecommerce experiences aren't likely to perform research and purchase via snail mail.

Overall, technology has made it easier to research and faster to respond to consumer demands for information and goods. It's not about "pushing" information out to prospects; now the prospects are "pulling" product information on their timeline and at their own convenience.

Duplication of Efforts and Lack of Alignment

In the past, MSCS were separate departments. After one department "finished" with a customer, they handed him or her off to the next department. Naturally, each department had its own way to measure performance, such as through conversion rates. In addition, each department had its own operations, analysis, and tools.

This duplication of effort often resulted in (and still results in) misunderstandings and friction among the departments. Furthermore, each department translated the high-level, go-to-market strategy into their own business processes, sometimes without a clear understanding of what the other departments were doing. This led to misalignment with other departments and a disconnect with the strategy.

Complexity from Increased Dependence on Software

Since 2011, the number of companies that create MarTech software (a blend of marketing and technology) has grown from 150 to over 5,000 in 2017. That's a 97% increase in just six years!

Furthermore, each department (Marketing, Sales, and Customer Success) probably uses several software tools each. That's at least 12 software programs to keep track of across MSCS.

The impact of all of this new technology has the following effects:

❖ You have to perform research regularly and diligently to remain aware of what software tools are available.

❖ Once you purchase the software, you have to learn it and understand how to best use it to get the maximum ROI.

❖ You must regularly install new versions, apply software patches, and back up data.

❖ You need to instruct end users on how to perform their job tasks using the software correctly and in line with the company processes.

That's a lot of keep up with!

It doesn't make sense for each department to have a technical person to manage their "set" of software (called a "tech stack"). Not only is there going to be some duplication of effort, because software often communications with other software, it's extremely important to be careful when applying software updates and other maintenance tasks. One wrong step can create a negative ripple across departments, causing a loss of data or a loss of software functionality.

New Roles of Marketing, Sales, and Customer Success

For better or worse, software and technology has changed MSCS.

It's empowering for customers to seek out their own information at their own pace. They may not literally walk through your "front door" ready to buy. Instead, they may pop-up on your website wanting to communicate with someone from your company via the chat application.

Customers are definitely aware of this new power. For example, instead of waiting in line at your brick-and-mortar store to return an item they didn't like, they might complain on a social media site about your poor product.

Marketing, Sales, and Customer Success always need to be monitoring their channels in order to be perpetually available to the customer, and those channels better be performing perfectly, or you're going to hear about it!

A Rev Ops department can be responsible for the entire tech stack used by MSCS, ensuring that at the technology level, all of the software is working and inter-communicating. This leaves the MSCS staff free to do what they were hired to do.

Marketing can not only just drive leads into the funnel; they can stay involved throughout the entire customer lifecycle. They can drive new business, but also apply their marketing efforts to the up-sell and cross-sell opportunities as well as churn prevention.

Instead of just receiving leads from Marketing and moving them through the sales funnel, Sales can spread awareness about the product and the brand using social media. With more data available to them, they can devise and initiate more effective outbound sales programs.

Customer Success can now be involved earlier in the process because they can see which leads are coming into the system. They can use the data that's been gathered to compare new customers to current ones and concentrate on those most likely to be open to additional purchases or longer subscriptions.

In fact, if you remove the duplication of roles and tasks in Marketing, Sales, and Customer Success, you can hire more marketing specialists, account executives, and customer success representatives. With the support of Rev

Ops, you can get those people up to speed quickly, thereby scaling that much faster.

How to Start Up Rev Ops at Your Company

If your company has over 100 employees, the tasks explained in this chapter are likely already being handled in separate departments (Marketing, Sales, Customer Success, and IT). To bring all of these responsibilities under one roof requires a leader, frequently referred to as Chief Revenue Officer (CRO).

If you don't have the situation described above, you can distribute the responsibilities between two employees, one who does Sales Ops and one who does Marketing Ops. You will eventually reach a point when these roles can be brought together into one role to start Rev Ops. This usually happens when projects and communication become more complex – the general consensus is about 100 employees.

Difficulties and Pitfalls

Because Rev Ops touches so many different parts of your revenue-generating areas, it increases the likelihood that things can go wrong. I've gone over a few of them in this section:

Rushing It

After you have a broad, go-to-market strategy and annual goals, take time to clearly define your sales processes… everything from the buyer's persona to the buying journey to the sales stages. From there you can design a sales process that matches the buying journey as closely as possible.

Make sure the sales process you create includes a consistent way to track performance. You want to be able to see the conversion rates from one sales stage to the next. Select key performance indicators (KPIs) that tell you how effective your sales processes are, then continue to tweak these processes. (I go over KPIs in Chapter 12.)

Not Yet Ready for Rev Ops

Rev Ops isn't going to be able to make progress if Marketing, Sales, and Customer Success are working by the seat of their pants, putting out fires every other day. Before Rev Ops can make a difference in revenue and scaling, a few things have to be put into place:

❖ Go-to-market strategy

❖ A reasonable goal (for example, the number of new subscriptions for the year)

❖ Formal, measurable sales process for generating and closing the right kinds of leads

When these components are in place and functioning well, Rev Ops can provide the support to keep MSCS aligned toward its goals. This can involve any number of enablement projects, such as marketing content, implementing a new sales tools, or tweaking existing sales processes for maximum efficiency.

Lack of Regular, Closed-Loop Communication

One of the best ways to meet your revenue goals is through regular, closed-loop meetings. I can just hear the groans out there for having to schedule "yet another meeting," but hear me out.

❖ First of all, you can't rely on those "water cooler" conversations to resolve problems. It's just not an effective place to raise an issue and plan to solve it.

❖ Secondly, if Rev Ops schedules a regular (say, weekly) meeting, you'll find you are getting MSCS problems resolved more quickly and having less impromptu hallway meetings, thus saving more time.

❖ Thirdly, if you don't meet and communicate regularly, any MSCS problem is going to get larger as time goes on. Gaps in communication can stretch into the Grand Canyon Communication Gap, making it harder to resolve problems.

Of course, Rev Ops is the one to schedule, run, and mediate these meetings, making sure they bring an agenda with the relevant data. It's best to have everyone in the same room; the next best option is a video conference call. This is the place to iron out any wrinkles in the sales process as well as identify or communicate needs.

Chapter Summary

With the growth of ecommerce through emerging technologies, consumers have become savvier and more sophisticated, managing their own research and making purchases at their convenience. Thankfully, technology has also provided better tools to the revenue-generating departments of a business as well as access to more and better data.

However, the new opportunities presented by ecommerce, savvy consumers, and technology also present a more complex landscape that can't be mastered if MSCS continues to operate in its traditional ways. The tools are only effective if MSCS understands how to use them most effectively. The data is only useful if they understand how to analyze and draw insights from it.

Rev Ops is an emerging role, especially for SaaS companies, to support the overarching and day-to-day responsibilities of Marketing, Sales, and Customer Success. Beyond just operational services to these departments, Rev Ops can provide the means for better communication among departments, breaking down the silos of information that can lead to broken processes and lost opportunities.

In terms of the number of MSCS employees, this may not be a role your company is ready for, but you can put into place some of the revenue-enhancing tasks by assigning them to one or two employees. Some of these tasks were mentioned in the "What Does Rev Ops Do?" section. Additional tasks include:

❖ Gathering the data to support next year's go-to-market strategy

❖ Defining the sales stages and related workflows

❖ Schedule, run, and mediate MSCS meetings to keep the lines of communication open

In establishing a high-performance sales team, what is some advice you would give to senior leaders in a company?

SCOTT LEESE

Let the sales leader participate and set realistic goals for the team instead of having private conversations with investors or the board and over-promising and then dropping the hammer on the sales leader to deliver. Give them operational support in the form of sales ops hires so they can focus more on strategy and coaching and development instead of reporting.

SAMAR BIRWADKER

Sales can be a tough gig, but it's also one of the most rewarding when you get it right. The advice I'd give senior leaders when establishing a high-performing sales team is to let them experiment. Don't tie them to one tactic or strategy because you never know what might move the needle quicker or more effectively until you give your team the autonomy to try a few things first.

RICHARD HARRIS

We remind executives of the undeniable value of participating first-hand in their own sales cycles. Only this will allow for best decisions to be made. The further away the executive is from the sales conversation, the harder it will be for them to make quality decisions.

Chapter 12 – The Plans (Strategic & Operational)

If you already have high-level goals in place for your business, that's great! Even better if you've detailed them in a strategic plan. To keep everyone focused and aligned around those goals, you need two more things: an *operational plan* and *a way to measure progress*.

I could write an entire book on strategic and operational plans (and I just might do that), but for now I'll provide a high-level overview (later in this chapter). The real focus of this chapter is on how you can track your progress toward strategic and operational goals by using key performance indicators (KPIs).

But before I get to that, I first need to make sure we're all on the same page by covering some information about strategic and operational plans.

Benefits of an Operational Plan

An operational plan explains how the company will go about fulfilling the goals and performing the activities outlined in the strategic plan. It's important for many reasons.

Keeps the Company on Track

While your company scales, an operational plan helps you stay on track by enforcing the same procedures, checklists, and so forth. It's fairly simple to run a tight ship when you're a handful of employees, but much more difficult if you scale up to 50 staff members. The operational plan helps to maintain the same quality of product (or service) no matter how large you get.

Adds Value to Your Business

Although you're probably not thinking about this now, the operational plan can make your business more valuable if you ever decide to sell it. Sellers will feel much more comfortable buying a business with established and documented procedures because they know they can run the company even if you're no longer around. This is a much better position to be in as a seller than having to admit that all of your company's procedures are stored precariously in your brain.

Serves As a Training Resource

Being able to hand a new employee your company's operational plan (or at least the part that affects them) is a great way to introduce them to your business. I'm not suggesting that this is the only way you indoctrinate new employees, but it can free up time otherwise spent explaining fundamental details.

Forces You to Be Consistent and Efficient

Writing down your procedures, policies, and checklists in black and white, you might notice discrepancies, issues, or inconsistencies. It has something to do with bringing them into the light of day in a structured way.

There's nothing wrong with this, and that's why I put it in the benefits section! Once you have your operational plan documented, you can iron out these problems and update your instructions accordingly.

Explains the Business to Employees

The operational plan can help employees better understand other areas of the company and why certain decisions are made. In that way, it can be empowering and inspire trust. The operational plan also makes it easier for employees to cross-train in other areas of the business or make suggestions for improvement.

Keeps Everyone Strategically Aligned

The strategic plan outlines the direction and activities a company will undertake for the next year. This may seem obvious, but an operational plan helps to align everyone in the organization to the strategic plan, even though they are probably involved in widely different activities. Your time and energy are better focused when you are all aligned.

Strategic Plan Versus Operational Plan

This section gives you a bit more information about strategic plans and operational plans.

Strategic Plan

A strategic plan outlines what the company intends to accomplish over the next year. (Some companies create strategic plans for the next 1 - 3 years or have a 3 - 5-year plan.) The leaders of a business work together to create the company's strategic plan.

Of all the activities a company could be doing and directions it could take, the strategic plan defines what activities and direction it *will* take. A strategic plan looks ahead to where it wants to be in terms of the marketplace, customers, and products.

Here are some examples of strategic objectives:

❖ Reduce expenses by 5% (financial efficiency objective)

❖ Increase customer retention (revenue objective)

❖ Link employee performance to incentives and rewards (cultural objective)

Other information that supports the company's strategic plan are:

❖ *Mission statement*—How a company describes it current activities.

❖ *Vision*—Sums up your company's idea of what it will be in the future.

❖ *Core values*—Your brand's character and what the company stands for, also described as your reason for being. (We covered this in Chapter 4.)

In order to look to the future and make plans, a company must have a clear idea of its current situation. To support the strategic plan, you should understand the competitors, the marketplace, and your competencies (a fancy way of defining what sets you apart from the competition).

Operational Plan

If the strategic plan describes "what we're going to do" then the operational plan explains "how we're going to do it." The purpose of an operational plan is to define how the company will achieve the objectives set forth in its strategic plan. The operational plan – which also goes by the name of *playbook* or *operations manual* – is the link between the high-level strategy and the lower-level, day-to-day tasks.

Because the operational plan serves as the means for measuring your company's progress toward its strategic goals, I've provided more detail about it in the next few sections.

What Goes into an Operational Plan?

Besides documenting a company's day-to-day procedures (which I mention in the next section), the operational plan needs to address how the high-level goals set in the strategic plan are going to be fulfilled. This is necessary because high-level objectives are not specific enough in themselves to give employees the direction needed to accomplish them.

For example, let's say you had a strategic objective to convert 5% more leads into customers for the upcoming year. The operational plan breaks this high-level strategic objective into mini-goals. One of these mini-goals might be to hire two new account executives. Another mini-goal might be to implement a new set of email templates. You get the idea. Each of those mini-goals can be broken down into separate steps.

What Else to Put in the Operational Plan

It's generally easiest to document procedures by starting at a high-level, such as writing down the input and output of a specific department. Then write down what gets monitored in that area, what gets created, who gets collaborated with, and so forth. This information helps you to come up with a more detailed list of a department's procedures.

Besides documenting the company's daily business operations (also known as standard operating procedures, or SOPs), an operational plan can include:

❖ Checklists (to cover those "things that must be done," such as when welcoming a new customer or discharging an employee)

❖ Situational "how to" guides (to help troubleshoot common problems)

❖ Customer policies (such as for refunds, exchanges, and so forth)

❖ Frequently used reference and support material, such as templates or forms used in procedures

❖ Contact list (for you, other employees, emergency numbers, etc.)

For the most part, these procedures can be written by the managers and employees who perform the tasks. As part of a regular weekly meeting, review a newly written procedure so that you don't develop a backlog that needs to be approved.

How to Keep the Operational Plan Alive

From the beginning, even if it's not entirely complete, you need to make the operational plan easily accessible to all employees. You may need to make it available both digitally and on paper. For the former, you can publish to a private intranet or company wiki. For the latter, you should print out the operational plan and place it in a three-ring binder.

Just as you introduce and constantly refer to your company's culture, you need to do the same with your operational plan. One of the biggest challenges after completing the operational manual is keeping it updated. If the plan becomes out-of-date, it's difficult to get employees to follow it, and you can't blame them.

Here are some ways you can keep the operational plan current:

❖ After hiring someone, have them read all the manuals and then give them a test on their understanding of the work they have to do. This reinforces the importance of the operational plan and saves you some time.

❖ When performing a procedure, an employee should either be viewing it on their computer monitor or have the pages open at their workstation. Not only does this reinforce the correct procedural steps, the employee can make a note of any steps or information that needs to be changed.

❖ To better deal with changes in procedures, establish a quick and simple way for employees to either update procedures themselves or inform a responsible person to make the change.

How to Measure Progress with KPIs

One of the challenges in working toward your goals is that you might not be quite certain if your tasks are going to help you reach your goals. Finding a way to measure progress along the way is crucial. That way, if it appears that your tasks are not helping you reach your goals fast enough or are moving you in the opposite direction, you can immediately make changes to fix this.

To measure progress on a regular basis, you can use KPIs – *key performance indicators*. A KPI is a measurement of either a current condition or past performance. You can use KPIs to measure progress and help predict the outcome.

The best KPIs are numerically quantifiable and not open to subjective input. Some examples of KPIs for website marketing are:

❖ *Website traffic*—Typically measured across a 24-hour period.

❖ *Page conversion rate*—The percentage of website visitors to a webpage that end up being converted into customers.

❖ *Time on site*—How many minutes or seconds a website visitor remains before leaving.

Obviously, KPIs will vary depending on what you are focusing on. The IT department will have different KPIs from Customer Success, which will have different KPIs from Human Resources, and so forth.

Commonly Used KPIs

Below is a list of KPIs that are commonly tracked at companies. Even if these are not related to a strategic objective, they're still extremely helpful metrics to follow.

KPI	To help track...

Customer Churn Customer Engagement Score Customer Health Score	Customer satisfaction and retention
CAC: LTV Ratio Customer Lifetime Value (LTV) Customer Acquisition Cost (CAC) Months to Recover CAC	Sales efficiency
Qualified Marketing Traffic Leads by Lifecycle Stage Lead-to-Customer Rate Revenue Churn	Marketing and Sales effectiveness

Select the Best KPIs for Your Goals

In general, you should have 2 - 3 KPIs for each strategic focus area. There are two types of indicators: lag (or lagging) and lead (or leading):

Lag Indicators

Lag indicators measure performance that has occurred in the past. One example of a lag indicator is Customer Churn (the customer attrition measurement).

A lag indicator is valuable in that it can show that a pattern is occurring. So, using our example of Customer Churn, if you saw your Customer Churn percentage was increasing week by week, you'd know you were in trouble.

The problem with using only lag indicators is that you're looking at the past, which you cannot change. Again, using the example of Customer Churn, by the time you're looking at Customer Churn for the previous month, it's already a done deal. It's certainly helpful information but looking at it doesn't tell us (until it's too late) if our corrective measures are working.

Lead Indicators

Lead indicators are a bit trickier to explain. They are also measurements, but they're usually more granular and are used to help you determine if you're going in the right direction. You can figure out your leading indicators by looking at what you can control in order to influence your desired outcome.

For example, to have less Customer Churn, you could track lead indicators like:

❖ Number of times logged in per week/month

❖ Amount of time logged in

❖ Number of missed payments

After you have changed some things in Customer Success, you could check these lead indicators on a weekly basis to discover if your changes have helped – or not. If your changes haven't helped, you can react quickly with adjustments. You are using lead indicators to be proactive about an issue.

Involve Employees with KPIs

It's important to select KPIs that your leaders and employees understand because they are the ones tasked with performing the day-to-day jobs that will meet your strategic objectives. A smaller business can have everyone meet to discuss and decide on which KPIs will be used. Larger organizations will need to limit participation to the company leaders, managers, and team leaders.

If employees cannot participate because of your company's size, you can still keep them informed of the progress of the KPI development. After all, these KPIs will have a direct effect on employee focus and motivation, so it makes sense to keep them involved as much as possible.

When you introduce the KPIs, whether they're company-wide, departmental, or individual, make sure you explain the reasoning behind selecting them. Employees must understand why you are using these KPIs and how focusing on them can help your business achieve its goals.

Companies can use technology to keep KPIs current and front-and-center by displaying the latest KPI metrics on large-screen monitors mounted throughout the facility. There is plenty of software available that enables employees to view company and personal KPIs on a virtual dashboard. In addition, as an agenda item at weekly meetings, you should discuss any KPI issues that have emerged.

Make sure you celebrate success when you meet a KPI goal. If a department or even the company fails to meet a KPI, don't ignore it. Address the issue by figuring out what went wrong and how you plan to fix it. In this way, you're modeling the behavior you expect out of your employees if they fail to meet a personal KPI goal.

Difficulties and Pitfalls

Let's go over a few things that can go wrong when working with operational plans and KPIs.

Using the Wrong Metrics

Make sure that the metrics you select are directly relevant to your high-level strategic objectives. Especially in Marketing and Sales, there's a tendency to get caught up in the wrong metrics, like website views or social media likes. Focusing on these types of "vanity metrics" can send you off on a wild goose chase by, say, working on the wrong things or chasing the wrong customer segment.

Another mistake is tracking something at too high of a level to give you helpful information. Take the overall website conversion rate. Knowing this doesn't really help you much. What's more helpful is to know the web pages that lead to conversion or the conversion rate by online traffic type.

Other ways in which you can get off-track with metrics are:

❖ Looking at the metrics out of context

❖ Having goals that are metrics-based

❖ Using metrics to compare team members or teams against each other

Ignoring the Operational Plan

Sometimes the work that was put into the operational plan gets linked with something negative in your mind. Maybe in thrashing through several procedures, some heated exchanges between employees took place. Maybe the CMO marked up your writing with a red pen, reminding you of your high school English teacher. Whatever the case, the result is that when you're done with the operational plan, you mentally put it on a shelf to gather dust.

Well, here's some tough love: if you let your operational plan lapse and it becomes outdated, you've really shot yourself in the foot. It's not just a matter of updating the material… now you'll not only have to rework a large chunk of material, you'll also have to *reintroduce* it to your employees and work it back into your culture.

Do yourself and your employees a huge favor and insist that the information in the plan remains up-to-date. If there were ever a good reason to hire an intern, this would be one of them.

Operational Plan Is Too Complex

There's such a thing as providing too much detail. Too much detail means more that you have to keep updated. It can also unintentionally put off employees who feel bogged down every time they try to follow the procedures.

If you think this is the case for your operational plan, you can look at these areas to help control unnecessary complexity:

Screen captures

When explaining software or related procedures, you don't need to capture every single screen.

Long paragraphs

Big blocks of text are difficult for our eyes to track. Wherever possible, use short paragraphs and add more headings and bulleted lists to create more white space on the page/screen.

Illustrations or video

An illustration with a red arrow is more succinct than explaining where the do-hickey is located. You can also use short video clips to explain a step or even a short task.

Repetitive text or repetitive ideas

You don't need to define a new term before every section, for example (just create a glossary and put all of your company's jargon and terminology in there.) It's also okay to reference previous procedures instead of repeating them. Just make sure you're not forcing employees to constantly flip from one procedure to another in order to complete a task.

Disconnect Between High Level Objectives and Low-Level Tasks

If it seems like you aren't getting any closer to reaching your strategic objectives, make sure your KPIs, goals, projects, and daily tasks all contribute to the high-level strategic goals. The department managers (or team leads) are the obvious one to help with this.

Managers or team leads must translate high-level strategic objectives into weekly goals and projects as well as help employees understand how their daily tasks fit in to the high-level strategic objectives. In addition, managers help employees set personal goals and provide coaching and feedback if it looks like an employee won't meet the goals that feed into the high-level objectives.

Chapter Summary

A strategic plan provides a framework in which you can scale your business. With all of the choices and directions available to you, it keeps you focused so that you don't waste energy, money, and time.

The operational plan is the "nuts and bolts" of the strategic plan. Besides addressing all of the everyday "how to" operating concerns, it defines exactly what is going to be done to accomplish the stated objectives in the strategic plan.

Think of the strategic plan as the destination on the map, and the operational plan highlights the path you'll take to get there. To help you get there, KPIs serve as supportive signs to help you get there efficiently and with fewer bumps in the road.

What's the biggest piece of advice you can give other entrepreneurs who are trying to scale and grow their business?

MIKITA MIKADO

Stay positive and know that no matter how difficult it gets, you're always learning. The worst failures are typically the best for learning and getting better at the craft.

BOB MARSH

For very early stage entrepreneurs, run as much of it yourself for as long as you can. Nobody can capture and communicate the vision like you can. For those who are further along, don't miss on the fundamentals of good management. As you grow, scaling will come down to the effective management of people.

Chapter 13 – Stay Fresh and Be Adaptable

Change is a funny thing, often viewed as an unwelcome, unexpected, and annoying visitor, something we "deal with" and then politely steered out the back door so that we can return to our regularly scheduled program.

Like that undesirable guest, change is often an external factor, such as when:

❖ The economy tanks

❖ Government regulations or laws demand it

❖ Your customers make it clear that their needs are changing

❖ The competitive landscape shifts

❖ An opportunity arises that you can capitalize on

I mention these external factors because I want you to recognize them when they appear. Change doesn't always announce itself with fanfare and trumpets.

I also think it's important to alter our normal perception of change as being a threat or something negative. Change is always occurring in our universe. While it's difficult to *always* view it as something positive, we can at least try to view it neutrally and learn how to expect and adapt to it.

Why It's Important to Remain a Flexible and Open to Change

A company that can remain lean and nimble will likely be able to adjust more quickly and easily to market changes (or any other change, for that matter). If you can adopt certain traits and habits (which I go into later), your business stands a better chance of being around many years down the road.

Remember Blockbuster? It was very good at what it did, but it did not take into account how quickly a niche idea like Netflix could spread. Although part of Blockbuster's success lay in the fact that it ran like well-oiled machine, that was also (ironically) its fatal flaw. It did not have a culture that was receptive to new ideas.

Netflix Versus Blockbuster

Netflix was born in 1997 as a mail-order DVD rental business with just 30 employees. It didn't have an easy time of it at first. In the year 2000, in the midst of the turbulent dot-com bubble era and still relying on the U.S. postal service for DVD deliveries, Netflix was losing money.

Netflix approached Blockbuster, the reigning king of a chain of brick-and-mortar DVD-video rental stores, with the offer to be bought out for $50 million. If the deal went through, Netflix would rename itself to Blockbuster and provide the same mail-order DVD rentals while Blockbuster managed the DVDs and stores.

Blockbuster refused. It considered Netflix a mere "niche" business, and one that was losing money at that. Although Blockbuster started some internet services in 2004, it was still heavily invested in its brick-and-mortar store model, evidenced by its attempted takeover of Hollywood Video in the same year.

In the early '00s, Netflix began to develop its idea of offering downloadable movies. By 2007 it had developed its streaming media delivery service.

Belatedly, Blockbuster realized the threat of Netflix and streaming media. It attempted to address some of its shortcomings, such as its much-maligned late penalty fees and began to offer streaming media. But Netflix had too much of a head start, and Blockbuster was always trying to play catch-up to Netflix.

Due in large part to its inability to change to meet its customers' needs, Blockbuster filed for bankruptcy in 2010. As of 2018, it planned to close its last brick-and-mortar store in Bend, Oregon.

While Netflix still offers DVD rentals via mail, it's more popular now for its television and movie streaming service, which is offered across the globe in nearly every country. Netflix is also gaining a reputation as a film production company for television series and movies.

When you consider that Netflix is now worth around $130 billion, the $50 million that it was willing to be bought out for in 2000 now seems like quite a deal.

The Lesson Behind Netflix and Blockbuster

Looking back on it, Netflix seems to have had the ability to see into the future. In reality, Netflix was just listening closely to what its customers wanted – and didn't want.

Some examples:

❖ Blockbuster customers didn't like having to fight the crowds and lines to get a movie; Netflix was born on the idea of online DVD rental with at-home delivery.

❖ Despite Blockbuster's popularity, its onerous late penalty fees were naturally despised by everyone. While Netflix couldn't deliver Blockbuster's instant gratification of in-person media rental, it *could* delight customers by not applying late fees.

❖ Inspired by their customers' complaints of damaged and scratched DVDs, in the early '00s, Netflix looked into technology that allowed customers to download movies online (streaming would come later).

Which Raises the Question of Survival

So how does a company become a smoothly-run, revenue machine while keeping its finger on the pulse of changing technology and marketplace *and* remaining open and responsive to its customers and new ideas? That's a tall order.

There's certainly no prescription for success, but there are certain traits and habits that a company can adopt to remain lean and nimble. Each business is as unique as an individual; therefore, you must find your own ways to apply the concepts I cover in this section.

Uphold the Entrepreneurial Attitude

An entrepreneur is a person who pursues profits by implementing new technology or strategies as well as offering innovative products or services. These entrepreneurial traits and behaviors can be encouraged at your company by including them in your workplace culture.

While being able to execute consistently and with excellence day after day is admirable (and imperative), it's equally important to look beyond your targeted objectives. Not everything that you observe will be relevant to your business, but this wider perspective can expand your field of opportunities.

The entrepreneurial attitude is much more than that, of course. The following sections summarize more of what you can grow and encourage in your own business.

Employees Can Help You Stay Current

Employees should not be penalized for taking calculated risks and experiencing failure. Make sure they have access to professional development, organizations, and associations that are appropriate for their roles; these are places where they can learn, network, and hear the latest news and developments in their industry. When they return from a professional event, ask them for their thoughts and what they have learned.

Embrace Technology

As much as possible for your industry and business type, look at how technology can help you understand your customers better. Currently, the latest trends are in data analytics, recommendation engines, machine learning, and AI. Companies are using the data they acquire from their omnichannel to personalize the customer experience. However, don't embrace technology just for the sake of technology; do it in a meaningful way.

Before jumping into any large-scale technology changes, first address any underlying issues in your network architecture and infrastructure. Make sure they can handle rapid changes and sudden, increased usage (such as when you launch a new app or campaign).

Accept Failures Along the Way

With the technology and the marketplace evolving so rapidly, it's more of a question of *when* you're going to stumble rather than *if.* As I mentioned earlier, it's a mistake to punish employees for mistakes or failures; it negates the whole learning process.

It's not that people shouldn't be held accountable for overall poor performance. They should have to answer for repeatedly disappointing behavior. What I'm talking about are the mistakes people make when they try new things or experiences. A failure might set one back a step or two, but you can regain what you've lost by examining the experience and applying the knowledge to future endeavors.

You can apply this to your overall business as well. A company that is heading in the right direction yet experiences a defeat or disappointment shouldn't become risk-averse and stagnate. To do so would be to ignore a huge lesson.

Revolve Your Business Around the Customer

Every company in the world gives lip-service to the promise of customer focus, support, and retention. In reality, though, customers' needs are often sacrificed on the altar of pursuing profit.

Trust me, I'm not deprecating the pursuit of profit, but a business that places profit first and customers second is putting itself in a precarious position. Some of the tactics below can help you better understand and serve your customers.

Build Relationships with Customers

If you're reading this book, then I believe you really are interested in building a business for the long term... not just to make a quick buck. Since that's the case, you need to consider how your business can build a relationship with a customer. If you're still a small company, this is easier to do than with a large corporation. You may already have a core set of customers who have been with you since the beginning – that's great! (But stick around in case you can pick up a few more good tidbits of information.)

Understand Customers

Besides researching customers, you can ask them questions to better understand why they purchased your product. The information you gather also makes the selling process easier.

This kind of conversation is best accomplished face-to-face; if you can't manage that, try a phone call. You might be tempted to handle this digitally but using email and fill-in forms make it impossible to ask the right follow-up questions that are based on the customer's previous answer.

Your sales staff are in a position to help better understand customers, which is why it's important that sales debrief after each customer engagement. All CRM software has a feature where you can record the details of customer encounters.

Customer Communication

You can't be around all the time or be the only one to communicate to your employees, so it's crucial that during onboarding you emphasize how you want employees to work with customers. You also need to establish a turnaround policy for returning customers' emails and voicemails.

Customer Feedback

If you ask for customer feedback (and you should), ensure that any negative feedback is addressed and communicated back to the customer. About requesting feedback, don't smother your customers with constant requests to "tell us how we're doing." If you are sending a request for feedback by email, you may need to experiment to find the best gap between the customer receiving the product/service and your feedback request.

Existing Customer Base

Don't forget that your existing customer base is valuable for two reasons: it's easier to sell to them than get new customers *and* loyal customers spread the word to others. Customer loyalty programs are a great way to show steadfast customers they're appreciated. Just try to do this in a way that doesn't make the customer jump through hoops in order to enjoy the rewards!

Emphasize Customer Retention

Although we as business people understand the value of our existing customers – can I just say it? – there's something vastly more alluring about "winning" new customers. That being said, the money you spend on creating a customer retention program and identifying at-risk customers is less than what you'll spend to acquire a new customer.

You can identify at-risk customers in many ways, such as the customer having a large number of open tickets (if your business is technology related) or the customer has frequently called to get help. These "squeaky wheel" customers may need more attention in the form of training or assistance with implementing the software.

Other ways to Identify "at risk" customers include tracking:

❖ How frequently a customer is using your product. If only infrequently, contact the customer and ask them why. They might just need a bit of retraining or another demo.

❖ Customers who have purchased or upgraded regularly and then suddenly change their habits. This is another reason to call the customer and find out their reason.

You should also contact customers who haven't purchased from you in a while to understand why they've stopped. If you've lost good customers, it still makes sense to try to get them back, especially if they did not show signs of dissatisfaction with your company (low or non-existent customer support calls, for example). What do you have to lose? (Nothing! You've already lost them once!)

Those Complaining Customers

Typically viewed as a pain in the neck, a complaining customer is a golden opportunity. If a customer has taken the time out of their day (even if it's only 30 seconds) to log a complaint with your company, it means they still want to be your customer (even if they say they don't). As for those customers who leave your business without a word to you, there are other ways to deal with them; I'll mention that later in this section.

Difficulties and Pitfalls

To quote Murphy's Law, "Anything that can go wrong will go wrong." That's why I have a "Difficulties and Pitfalls" section in so many of these chapters. Read this section to head off any of the more common mistakes and wrong turns.

Leaders Who Resist Change

Change at a company is usually introduced and championed by upper management. But that pendulum can swing quite far in the other direction if you find some of your company leaders are resisting change.

Of course, you must first determine *why* they don't want to change. You can't do anything until you determine why. The reason might be valid and based on information you aren't aware of. Sometimes the reasons can be surprising, having little if anything to do with your business or more to do with the inherent characteristics or past experiences of the person.

Employees Who Resist Change

Use the same advice as above and determine why employees are resisting change. It could be they don't like to learn new software or don't have confidence that the change will lead to a positive outcome. Exploring the reasons behind employee resistance can often yield very interesting results: things you didn't know that you should have known. Just like customer complaints, employee resistance can be valuable in unearthing new information.

Neglecting to Manage the Change Itself

The change you're introducing might be a new piece of state-of-the-art equipment. It could be a new department to help handle the growth of your company as it rapidly scales. Besides dealing with the thing itself that is bringing in change, such as the new equipment or new department, you must also manage how the change occurs.

Make sure you consider how each of your organization's areas will be affected by the change. Even if you think an area won't be affected, it's best to double-check rather than receive a rude surprise later. Once you know who is affected by the change, you can determine a plan for introducing it, preparing training, and so forth.

Making Assumptions

Some of the best laid plans have failed due to assumptions. If you performed your research and found you had adequate resources to support a change, make sure you recheck these facts when you get closer to implementation. The business world and marketplace changes so rapidly that in the months between making a decision and implementing it, your resources might have dried up or been allocated elsewhere.

The same warning applies to communication and coordination. Don't assume that the group who performed a service for you before is in sync with you and following along with the change. Poor communication and coordination have sunk many promising ventures.

Using the Wrong or Inadequate Technology

Some organizations take pride in bootstrapping it, even to the extent that their employees or projects suffer for lack of the proper software or hardware tools. Don't be that company. Make sure that either you or your leaders look into what tools are needed to support the proposed change.

You might flinch at the cost of new or updated software, but if it can help you get the job done faster or better, in the long run you are saving money. If the hardware you've been using has been free of problems for the last ten years, its age alone – and Murphy's Law – should be enough to make you suspicious of it. Don't depend on any one piece of hardware alone to carry the success of a project. Either buy new or have a Plan B ready just in case.

Chapter Summary

Whether change is forced upon your business because of external factors or because of your own internal drive to succeed and improve, you need to learn to manage it. Acting proactively instead of reactively is a step in the right direction. Also, whenever you feel yourself resisting change, say to yourself, "Remember Blockbuster!"

Some traits and habits are automatic or habitual with entrepreneurs, who must adapt quickly as they grow from a one-person business to a small business to an IPO. Some entrepreneurial traits and habits are easier than others to adapt for your own organization. They can include:

❖ Keeping employees current

❖ Embracing technology

❖ Accepting failure

❖ Being completely customer-focused

You'll need to adjust to company leaders or employees who are resistant to change. Instead of meeting the resistance with impatience, try to determine what is truly driving their opposition. You might discover something new that you need to address or help you transition.

Accommodating change is a challenge in its own right; you can't underestimate how it will affect the people you work with. You also can't be too careful in determining who the change actually affects. Only by knowing the extent of the change can you make sure you have the right strategy and resources in place to meet it.

In times of difficulty, how have you kept your focus on the vision for your company?

MIKITA MIKADO

Clarity, honesty, and lots of communication!

BOB MARSH

I get in front of customers. There's nothing like really learning about your client's business and understanding how what you do fits in to how they operate. This brings tremendous insight on where you can help your clients more, either through improved service or product ideas. I learned early in my career that when you're out in the field meeting with people, good things happen.

Chapter 14 – Final Words (For Now)

After reading this book, I hope that you have an overall better understanding of what it takes to move your business to the next level of success. Everything included in this book I consider "key" to successfully scaling a business.

The primary reason I wrote this book is because I want entrepreneurs and businesses to focus on the right things in preparing to scale their companies. If you have read through this book, I'm sure you've recognized at least a few areas that need improvement.

One of the most difficult decisions to make in running a business is knowing what aspect of it needs attention the most. If you're not sure how to prioritize these improvement areas, I suggest rereading the relevant sections from this book and weighing the pros and cons of working on each area.

After that, if you're still not sure and you're not ready to hire a consultant, you can join a peer group organization that provides its members with information and resources to help them grow their companies. These organizations exist across the globe, and some even specialize in certain industries, like technology.

If You Remember Anything, Remember This

This book contains a lot of information, and here's how I suggest you remember the most important points of this book, which has four main sections around these topics:

1. Culture

2. Employees

3. Sales

4. Strategy

Think of these of the stars of a movie. They're prominent, easily recognizable, and they shine when they're at their best. I've covered each of these stars in a separate chapter.

In a movie, the stars need supporting actors, right? So, let's layer those in:

1. **Culture**—Supported by Story, Brand, and Values.

2. **Employees**—Supported by P.h.D., Investing in Employees, and Performance Management.

3. **Sales**—Supported by the Sales Team, Knowing Sales Efficiency, and Rev Ops.

4. **Strategy**—Supported by Operational Plan/KPIs and Adaptability.

Each of these supporting players has a role… very important roles, too. Imagine workplace culture without a background story, branding, and core values; it would be a very dull and uninspiring place to work. And just *try* to have an effective strategy without an operational plan.

Of course, each of those supporting roles has its own chapter as well.

In Conclusion…

I'd love to hear from you, especially if you loved the book and even if you have some suggestions for material I need to cover for my next one. There are several ways to connect with me, so check out the "About the Author" section at the end of this book.

I stated this in the introduction, but it's so important I'll say it again. This is what I believe, and it hasn't steered me wrong yet:

#1 It all comes down to enjoying every minute of what you do.

#2 The key to leadership is enabling others to be the best they can be and supporting them along the way.

#3 The key to success is having *passion, hustle, and drive* **in everything you do.**

When you add 1, 2, and 3 together, there is no limit to how much you can grow yourself and your business!

Chapter-by-Chapter Summary

I've gone over a ton of material in this book, so in this section, I've recapped the main points for each chapter. Use this section as a refresher from time to time. Also, don't forget that there is a chapter summary at the end of each chapter that provides a more detailed overview.

Chapter 1 – Is It Time to Scale?

Make sure you figure out if you have a business model that can scale without incurring prohibitive costs that eat up your revenue. You need sales and marketing activities that are efficient and repeatable enough to ensure a strong income flow as you scale up. Use technology to reduce time-wasting activities and begin delegating more day-to-day tasks to responsible employees or freelancers so you can focus on the strategic side of your business.

Chapter 2 – It's All About the Story!

Using a story is a way to communicate a lot about your business without a lot of words. In fact, stories are so familiar to people that they're an immediate attention-getter. But you can't just throw something together and hope it'll work. A well-written story has these five elements: circumstances, curiosity, characters, conversation, and conflict.

Chapter 3 – Build Your Brand

Your company's brand is the platform you'll use for connecting with customers and prospects. It's just as valuable as your reputation, so make sure you put a hefty amount of time and attention into developing it. That's half the job.

The other half includes the activities around branding. If you can find helpful ways to engage with people who are interested in or use your product (or service) – instead of just bragging about how great you are – you'll find your brand recognition increasing more naturally as opposed to jamming it down people's throats.

Chapter 4 – Establish Your Core Values

Core values are like road signs that help guide your organization's journey. Both employees and customers pay attention to your core values because overall, society is more interested in doing business with companies that have developed and communicated their intentions. Obviously, these intentions (core values) need to be something beyond just raking in the cash. Don't try to "fake it" though, because nowadays consumers can easily spot phonies!

Chapter 5 – Become Culturally Aware

A business that has defined and promoted a positive workplace culture has many advantages over its competitors. An upbeat and encouraging culture at work attracts new talent and engages employees, which helps to keep job turnover low. If your culture is in tune with your core values and brand (as it should be), it enhances your company's reputation amongst customers. There's also evidence to support that organizations with a positive workplace culture have higher operating incomes and more satisfied customers.

Chapter 6 – Only Hire P.h.D.'s

When it comes to hiring your company leaders and employees, I'll always come back to *passion*, *hustle*, and *drive* (P.h.D.). In fact, I've already stated that I believe it's more important to hire based on P.h.D. than on job skills or experience. Although you may balk at having to train someone who has never, say, been an account executive before, you'll get so much more energy, excitement, and motivation out of a P.h.D. than a sophisticated AE who's been there, done that.

Chapter 7 – Invest in Your People

Once you have those awesome employees, you have to keep an eye on them... but not for the reason you're thinking! Your P.h.D. employees aren't slackers, but unless they are engaged at work, feeling challenged, and gaining new experiences/knowledge, they're going to look elsewhere for mental stimulation.

I'm talking about training and professional development, and you're not going to provide it just for the employees' benefit, but also for your company's. Seriously, there are too many benefits to list here, but a few of them include lower employee acquisition costs, higher productivity, and better adaptability to market/economy changes.

Chapter 8 – Set Expectations with Performance Management

Mention the words "performance management" and you'll likely clear the boardroom, breakroom, or whatever room you happen to be standing in. Perhaps due to bad experiences with such programs, many entrepreneurs and even some CEOs put performance management at the bottom of the list when it's time to scale.

It may help if you can understand that performance management is just a more formalized way for tracking and communicating the expectations you have around your employees' job functions. If you have any hope of meeting your strategic goals, it's through the efforts of your employees... so why wouldn't you want to know how well (or how poorly) they're doing on a regular basis?

Working performance management into your company's culture as a "given" and your P.h.D. employees will accept it. They'll benefit from clearly understanding their responsibilities, and you'll reap the benefits of better alignment, better personnel decisions, and better job performance.

Chapter 9 – Build a Winning Sales Team

It's pretty obvious why I wrote a separate chapter on hiring a winning sales team. You can't skimp on time or attention when hiring for sales, especially when hiring the wrong people can cause so much damage in terms of bad morale and additional employee acquisition costs. Besides making good hiring decisions for sales, your efforts should also go into having a sales playbook as well as proper onboarding and training.

Chapter 10 – The Economics of a Sale – Get It Right!

This chapter covers some crucial information needed to understand if your sales process is efficient enough to scale your business. I went over Lifetime Value (LTV), Customer Acquisition Cost (CAC), and the LTV/CAC Ratio. Another important one is the CAC Payback. And of course, you can't neglect the Churn Rate!

I didn't throw all this information at you to freak you out, but to point out that there's a very methodical, logical way to approach marketing and sales. Looking at your customer costs and revenue in this way keeps you focused on the crucial cash flow and how to optimize it.

Chapter 11 – Unite Your Sales Force Through Rev Ops

The Revenue Operations (Rev Ops) team is central to the success of your business because it brings the execution factor to your company's go-to-market strategy. By providing tools, insights, and processes to Marketing, Sales, and Customer Success (MSCS), Rev Ops enables MSCS to perform the all-important job of generating leads, closing sales, and retaining the customer base. In our fast-moving, tech-based business world, it's difficult to scale without centralizing all of the sales-related software, data, reports, and data analysis.

Chapter 12 – The Plans (Strategic & Operational)

If you don't have a strategic plan and its smart sibling, the operational plan, then you are simply reacting to day-by-day events with a fleeting thought of "goals" as you run to put out the latest fire. This might sound harsh, but with the fast pace of business and hungry competitors biting at your heels, you need to focus all your funds, employees, and energy in *one* direction. Getting your crew organized around the strategic/operational plans is how you'll accomplish that.

To know if your efforts are paying off, track them with some thoughtfully considered *key performance indicators* (KPIs). If you consistently communication your plans and involve employees in tracking KPIs, you find that – more often than not – your business is meeting its strategic objectives!

Chapter 13 – Stay Fresh and Be Adaptable

Change is going to happen, so you might as well accept it and be ready to roll with it. Easy as that is to say, it can be difficult to keep all those plates spinning while you systematically scan the horizon for changes in the landscape. Remember Blockbuster? Complacent in its success, it didn't realize the Netflix threat until it was too late. Don't be a Blockbuster!

Ensure your survival by maintaining an entrepreneurial attitude in your workplace culture. If you give employees learning opportunities via professional development, they can help your business keep up with competitors and the changing times. Don't penalize them for making mistakes based on calculated and informed risks. Remain alert for ways in which technology is going to change your business, your industry, and your customers.

Speaking of your customers, you probably know better than to just pay lip-service to being "customer focused," but since these are my final words (for now), I'll remind you again that today's consumers know what's real and what's phony.

Build solid relationships with customers by working to understand them and their changing needs. Don't feel threatened by their complaining or negative feedback. Pay special attention to those who look like they might be leaving your business; you might be able to bring them back, or if not, be able to learn something new from them. If you're a truly adaptable business, you'll actually be thrilled to learn something from a disenchanted customer!

If there was one message that you could get out to the world, what would it be?

MIKITA MIKADO

Communicate and try to empathize instead of fighting, resenting, hating.

BOB MARSH

In the context of modern selling, we must not forget the fundamentals. Far too many companies are putting too much energy and money into technology thinking they can automate and optimize everything. But we can't forget that the fundamentals of selling haven't changed – you have to call people, talk to people, uncover sales opportunities, move them through the sales process, and close business. And as a manager, you need to ensure those fundamentals are executed upon consistently and effectively. If you aren't getting those basics done well, you won't scale and no piece of technology to automate steps is going to make up for it.

What's one book that you would recommend that helped you scale your company faster?

MIKITA MIKADO

I'd recommend *Quiet Leadership,* by David Rock. It is a book that talks about leadership and management from the psychology and neuroscience angles. My "left" brain definitely dominates my right brain, and I'd say I don't have a naturally high EQ (emotional intelligence). Learning about what people feel from an analytical and logical standpoint helped to build a gateway into the world of organizational behavior, psychology, and emotional intelligence, which is what I'm trying to get better at today.

BOB MARSH

The Four Disciplines of Execution, by Sean Covey. This is a business classic and breaks down the keys of management into four basic principles. I think these are crucial to effectively lead a company or to manage an individual team.

The four disciplines are pretty simple:

Focus on the Wildly Important—Clearly define the outcome you want. For example, $10 million in sales.

Act on Lead Measures—Identify the controllable behaviors and actions that will lead to achieving that goal. For example, build $40 million in pipeline across 1,100 unique sales opportunities ($40 million divided by $25k average deal size), get salespeople to have 2,500 intro meetings, etc.

Keep a Compelling Scoreboard—Take the goal and the leading indicators and create simple to understand reporting that everyone can view so they know where they stand and where they need to increase focus at any time.

Create a Cadence of Accountability—Have a regular schedule for management to review performance against the scorecards and use that information to guide individual coaching. Adjust as needed.

YOU GOT THAT P.h.D.?

Contributors

THANK YOU MIKITA, SCOTT, RICHARD, BOB, SAMAR & KYLE!

I want to take a moment to thank the following guest contributors that shared their insights in scaling a business! Your feedback is greatly appreciated by me and will be very beneficial for the readers of this book.

MIKITA MIKADO

An entrepreneur, geek, and surfer who enjoys meeting new people and travelling. Co-founder of PandaDoc and Quote Roller. Born and raised in Minsk, Belarus; citizen of the planet Earth.

SCOTT LEESE

Leese is the Senior Vice President of Sales at Qualia, which has built the first settlement system in the title industry that takes advantage of modern technology. It specializes in working with owners to help close more transactions, get rid of repetitive data entry, and reduce errors.

In 2016 Leese founded his own consulting firm, Scott Leese Consulting, LLC and works across the country providing sales training, workshops, and motivational speeches to startups. He also serves as a Strategic Advisor to numerous startups domestically and abroad. In addition, he wrote a book on sales, *Addicted to the Process*, that was released in 2017.

Spending his entire professional career building and scaling sales organizations at SaaS companies, Leese has experience that includes a vast knowledge of online media, social media, marketing, lead generation, and advertising, with specific expertise in local advertising in the SMB market. He has a proven track record of lifting organizations to new heights with limited resources allocated to the task at hand.

RICHARD HARRIS

Harris is a seasoned SaaS sales leader and provides full-funnel sales training for SDR, AE, and Customer Success. He applies his knowledge from 20+ years of experience to helping early stage and expansion stage startups build their sales infrastructure and train their sales teams to "get there faster."

Harris has received the following awards and recognition:

- ❖ Top 25 Inside Sales Leader, Sales Trainer, Sales Hacker, Public Speaker, Advisor

- ❖ 2017, 2016, and 2015 AA-ISP's TOP 25 Most Influential Inside Sales Professionals

- ❖ Named to 40 Most Inspiring Leaders by SLMA

BOB MARSH

Marsh has spent his career in sales and sales leadership, because that's what he loves. As the EVP of Sales at Bluewater Technology, he works with a team of 250+ experts to help brands tell their stories through technology.

Most recently, he was the founder and CEO of LevelEleven, which is a sales management system used by some of the world's most progressive sales organizations, including HP Enterprise, Comcast Business, CarGurus, Verizon, and hundreds of others.

Prior to that, Marsh was a key salesperson and sales leader at ePrize, which was a fast-growing success story in metro-Detroit. As one of ePrize's first sales people, he helped to scale it to the 400+ person, unprecedented leader in the digital engagement marketing industry. At ePrize he was able to secure and grow top customers, including General Mills, Ford, General Motors, Target, and Delta Airlines.

Through building two category-creating businesses, he's had the opportunity to speak at several industry-leading events, including

Dreamforce, SaaStr, and Inbound. Marsh has been published in *Fast Company*, *Inc.com*, *Quotable*, and the *Harvard Business Review*.

As a competitive golfer in college, Marsh has it in his head that he could still be pretty good but would rather hang with his family and help build successful companies.

SAMAR BIRWADKER

Birwadker is the CEO of Good&Co, which was acquired by StepStone GmbH. He's also worked at AKQA and Landor Associates. He describes himself as a serial connector-of-dots, innovation consultant, and motohead.

KYLE PORTER

Porter is the founder and CEO of SalesLoft. SalesLoft generated explosive growth over the past two years, serving nearly 2,000 clients while tripling revenue in 2016. Porter led the team from four employees in 2014 to over 175 in 2016, and SalesLoft was named one of Atlanta's best places to work in surveys by the Atlanta Business Chronicle. Porter was also nominated for Atlanta Business Chronicle's Most Admired CEOs for 2017.

As a champion for organizational health and the Atlanta technology ecosystem, Porter is dedicated to helping SalesLoft's employees accomplish their goals and dreams, which is reflected in its extremely high ratings on GlassDoor.com. He is a frequent speaker at national conferences on the topic of leadership, fostering culture in a dynamic market, and modern sales.

Porter is a Georgia Tech graduate who loves wakeboarding, reading, cycling, and spending time with his wife April, daughter Brooklyn, and son, Clark Everett.

About Bobby

Bobby Marhamat loves spending his days with business leaders who are working to achieve success in scaling their companies. He looks forward to meeting people who want to do better in life, matching actions to their words. One of his many goals in life is to help employees improve their skills and confidence so that they can crush it in whatever they want to do.

Currently, Bobby is CEO of Linxx, a technology company. He has been working with technology companies for 20 years, using his experience with sales, marketing, revenue, and operations to help leaders scale their businesses across their organizations.

Besides enjoying technology at work, Bobby has fun tinkering with home automation and his vegetable garden. (He's known for his hot peppers.) To combine his love of home automation and gardening, he's intent on programming his outdoor irrigation system to water based on the local rain forecast.

Once the watering system is working flawlessly, Bobby can indulge in his other passions – traveling and reading. He's also the author of two other books: *Trying to Keep My Business from Being Left Behind in this Social Media World* and *The "B" Word: Becoming Foolishly Bold in Creating the Ultimate "Brand."* Bobby's business articles often appear online for Forbes, Social Media Today, LinkedIn, and his own website.

Prior to joining Linxx, Bobby worked at Revel Systems as COO. He has also held other leadership positions as CEO, CRO or VP of Sales in technology companies such as: Highfive, Limos.com, EVO², Verizon Wireless, LookSmart, ServerPlex Networks, and Sprint/Nextel. He is a contributing member of the *Forbes Business Development Council*, an invitation-only organization for senior-level sales and business development executives.

To learn more about Bobby, like his penchant for Oreo ice cream, you can visit his website (https://bobbymarhamat.com/) or follow him through any of these social media accounts:

Facebook: https://www.facebook.com/bobbymarhamat/

Twitter: https://twitter.com/bobbymarhamat

LinkedIn: https://www.linkedin.com/in/bobbymarhamat/

And Remember:

If you ain't making waves, you ain't kicking hard enough.

www.ingramcontent.com/pod-product-compliance
Lightning Source LLC
Chambersburg PA
CBHW060525210326
41521CB00023B/2348